KT-512-161

The Lion
Storyteller Bible

The Lion
Storyteller
Bible

Retold by
Bob Hartman

Illustrations by Susie Poole

LION
Children's Books

For the children of Emmanuel

Text copyright © 1995 Bob Hartman
Illustrations copyright © 1995 Susie Poole
This edition copyright © 2001 Lion Publishing

The moral rights of the author and illustrator
have been asserted

Published by
Lion Publishing plc
Sandy Lane West, Oxford, England
www.lion-publishing.co.uk
ISBN 0 7459 2921 4 (hardback)
ISBN 0 7459 3607 5 (paperback)
Lion Publishing
4050 Lee Vance View, Colorado Springs,
CO 80918, USA
ISBN 0 7459 2921 4 (hardback)

First hardback edition 1995
10
First UK paperback edition 2001
10 9 8 7 6 5 4 3 2 1

All rights reserved

Acknowledgments
Thanks to Su (for her encouragement, support and patience), to
Susie (for her wonderful lines and shapes and colours), and to
Lois (for the Easter basket). Thanks finally to God and my family.

A catalogue record for this book is available
from the British Library

Library of Congress CIP data applied for

Printed and bound in Spain

Contents

The New Testament

Introduction

From my experience as a pastor, parent and children's author, I realize that there are already many children's Bibles available. So I want to tell you what makes *The Lion Storyteller Bible* special. And I want to share with you several hopes I have for this book.

First, I hope that it will bring you closer to the children in your life. This book is meant to be read aloud—shared with an audience of children or grand-children or nieces and nephews, with a class at school or a church children's group. That's how many of the Bible stories were handed down to us in the first place: shouted by prophets, proclaimed by preachers, whispered as prayers—spoken out loud by one person to another. People were brought together by those words. They asked questions, shared insights or simply wondered together at God's love and power.

Next, I hope this book will help you to become a better storyteller. In my work as a storyteller for The Pittsburgh Children's Museum I am always amazed by the power of a story well told to capture and entertain and delight. I re-wrote the Bible stories in this book not so much to be read as to be told. I worked hard to be faithful to the original narrative, but I also included some storytelling devices—repetition, rhythm, and so on—so that the stories would land well on the listening ear.

What remains is for you, the storyteller, to supply the voice. And so I encourage you to familiarize yourself with the stories before you read them out loud. Discover the theme-threads I have woven to tie each story together. Make up different voices for the characters.

Come up with some noises or actions of your own. But above all, have fun with these stories. For that is the best guarantee that your children will enjoy them too.

I hope that, if you are a first-time storyteller sharing these retellings with one or two children at bedtime, these storytelling tips will be useful. If you are telling stories to a bigger group, why not look at the notes at the back of this book? There you will find some suggestions for simple participative storytelling.

Finally, a story Bible, by its very nature, requires the selection of certain stories and the omission of others. In this case, the stories have been chosen because they demonstrate, in terms young children will understand, that God is love. My hope as a Christian is that, having seen God at work from creation to the resurrection of Jesus, your children will learn to trust God and to listen for God's voice. And to love God in return.

Bob Hartman

Stories from the
Old Testament

In the Beginning

At first, there wasn't anything at all. Nothing! So God set to work. But he didn't use his hands, or a special machine. He spoke, that's all. He said, 'I'd like some light.' And there was light. Brighter than a summer morning or a thousand Christmas candles.

God spoke again. He said, 'Sky. I'd like some sky. And some water underneath.' And, sure enough, there it was. The bright blue sky. With the dark blue heavens above it. And the blue-green sea below.

'Earth.' That's what God said next, hard and firm, as if he really meant it. And the blue-green waters parted, and there was dry land underneath. Great patches of it, dirt black and brown. Here and there, all over the world.

'We need some colour,' God whispered, as if he were thinking out loud. And, quivering with excitement, green growing things crept right up out of the dark earth, then burst into blossom—red, orange and blue! Pine trees and palm trees. Rose bushes and blackberry bushes. Tulips and chrysanthemums.

God shouted next.

'Day—shining sun!'

'Night—shining moon!'

'Bright shining stars!'

And there they were, for morning and evening, summer and winter—time and heat and light!

After that, God called to the sky, as if he were expecting some kind of an answer.

'Come forth, flying things!' he called.

And through the clouds they came. Flying high and flying low. Flying large and flying small. Eagles and insects. Hummingbirds and hawks.

Then God called to the sea.

'Come forth, splashing things!'

And they came to him, too, leaping right up through the waves. Sailfish and swordfish. Dolphins and trout. Great grinning hump-backed whales.

Finally, God called to the earth.

'Come forth, walking things, crawling things, running, hopping, climbing things!'

And sure enough, they came. Up from burrows. Down from trees. Out of the high grass, and across the open plains.

Now everything was ready. Good and ready. So God spoke again.

'Man and woman,' is what he said, as if he were calling the names of his very best friends.

And out of the dust came Adam and Eve. To enjoy all that God had made. To take care of it for him. And to talk with him.

'This is the way things ought to be,' God said at last. 'This is good!'

A Sad Day

'Welcome to my world!' God said to Adam. 'It's good, isn't it?'

'Welcome to my garden!' God said to Eve. 'This is the most beautiful place of all. And I want it to be your home. Take care of the animals for me. Take care of the plants. And eat whatever you like. There are plenty of trees to pick from.'

Adam and Eve didn't know what to say. They looked at the garden. They looked at each other. And then they smiled the world's first smile.

Life was going to be perfect here. Just perfect.

'There's just one more thing,' God said. 'Do you see that tree over there? The one in the middle of the garden? Well, the fruit on that tree is not good for you. If you eat it, you will make me very unhappy. And you will have to leave this beautiful place.'

Adam and Eve looked at each other again. With so many trees to chose from, that hardly seemed to be a problem. And for a long time, they were content with soft juicy pears, sweet thick-skinned oranges, and round ripe melons.

Then, one day, the serpent came to visit.

'Tell me,' the serpent said to Eve, 'which trees are you allowed to eat from?'

'Every tree!' Eve smiled. 'Except the one in the middle of the garden.'

'Oh?' said the crafty serpent. 'And why is that?'

'Because it would make God unhappy,' Eve answered. 'And we would have to leave this beautiful place.'

'Ridiculous!' laughed the serpent. 'God does not want you to eat that fruit because he knows it would make you as clever as him. You know all about being good. But God has told you nothing about what it means to be bad. Eat the fruit, and you will know all about that, too!'

Eve thought that the fruit looked delicious. She had sometimes wondered what it tasted like. And it wasn't really fair of God to keep things from them.

So she picked a piece. And took a bite. And gave Adam a taste as well.

And, right away, they discovered what it meant to do something bad. Their stomachs churned with guilt. Their faces turned red with shame. And instead of running to meet God when he next visited the garden, they ran away to hide.

'I know what you have done,' God called out sadly. 'Now you will have to leave this beautiful place.'

'Goodbye,' God said to Adam. 'From now on, you will have to scratch at the earth for the food you eat.'

'Goodbye,' God said to Eve. 'Your life will be hard, too.'

'And when your lives end,' God said finally, 'you will go back to the ground from which you came.'

Adam and Eve looked at each other. Then they walked sadly out of the garden. They had learned what it means to be bad. And they had changed God's good world for ever.

A Special Promise

God was sad. Very sad. Everywhere he looked, he saw people making bad choices. Hating each other. Hurting each other. Making a mess of his beautiful world.

'I need to start all over again,' God decided. 'I need to make my world clean.' And that's when he talked to Noah.

Noah was not like the rest. He was a good man, and God knew it. So God told him to build a boat. A boat big enough to hold:
Noah,
his wife,
his three sons,
their wives,
a pair of every animal in the world,
and food enough to feed all of them for a very long time!

Noah's family was surprised when he told them what he was going to do.

Noah's neighbours thought it strange of him to build a boat so far from the sea.

And it wasn't easy chasing, and catching, and cleaning up after all those animals.

But Noah was a good man. He did what God told him—even when it was hard.

At last, when they were all tucked safely away in the boat, God shut the door. And then it started to rain.

It rained for forty days.

It rained for forty nights.

It rained harder than Noah had ever seen it rain before.

It rained so hard that the streams, and the rivers, and even the seas burst their banks and began to flood. Soon every sandy beach, every rocky path, every patch of muddy earth had disappeared beneath the water.

And the boat began to float.

It floated above the houses. It floated above the trees. It floated above the hills, and then above the mountains, too.

It floated for days and weeks and months.

And then it stopped, stuck at the top of a tall mountain.

Noah opened a window to look out. The water was going down, but the world was far from dry.

So he sent out a dove. And when the dove did not come back, Noah knew that it had found a dry place to build its nest.

'Come out!' God called, finally. 'Come out of the boat! The world is dry. The world is clean. And now you and your family and all the animals must have children and fill it full of life again!'

'Hooray!' Noah celebrated. And he thanked God for saving him.

God was happy, too. So he painted the world's first rainbow in the sky—to celebrate his fresh, clean world. And to promise that he would never send a flood like that again.

The Tall Tower

God looked. Something was happening in the land of Shinar.

God listened. And this is what he heard:

'Hey, you,' called a tall man. 'Throw me a brick.'

'Here you go,' snorted a short man, 'and could you pass me that axe?'

From all over the world, they had come—tall people, short people, fat people, thin people, all kinds of people. And they were building a tower!

Up, up, up they went. Stirring mortar. Making bricks. And hauling them high into the sky.

It was a big job. It was hard work. So it was a good thing they all spoke the same language—at least they could understand each other.

God looked and God listened again. This is what he heard:

'Say,' asked a fat man, 'why are we building this tower, anyway?'

'It's simple,' grinned a thin man. 'When we are finished this will be the tallest tower in the whole world.

'People will pass by, look at it and be amazed. We'll be more famous than the greatest king. We'll be more important than God himself!'

Now when God heard that, he jumped! And then he smiled.

'More important than me?' he chuckled. 'We'll see about that.'

That's when God decided to play the world's first trick. Did he wave his hand? Did he say some special words? Or did he just think it into happening? No one knows. But the next time God listened, this is what he heard:

'Hey, you,' called the tall man, 'pass me some mortar.'

'Fortwort?' snorted the short man. 'Hort mort a bortle.' (Which means something like, 'What did you say? I can't understand you.')

God chuckled again. He was enjoying this. So he listened some more.

'Excuse me,' asked the fat man, 'could I borrow your hammer?'

But the thin man didn't have a clue what he meant. 'Hub-wub?' he said. 'Flub-bub-a-gubble.' (Which means something like, 'What?')

And so it was, all over the tower. Instead of one language, there were suddenly hundreds. The workers couldn't understand each other. How could they go on?

So down, down, down they climbed, dropping their tools as they went. Then they babbled off in every direction, leaving the tower half-finished, half-done.

And whenever people passed by they were not amazed. No, some sniggered, some pointed, and some even said, 'Flep-nepp. Shlepp-rep-a-zepp.' (Which means something like, 'See, those men weren't more important than God, after all.')

God's Friend

Abraham was rich. He had lots of servants, to do his work for him. He had lots of camels and sheep. And he lived in a very nice place called Haran.

One day, God spoke to Abraham.

'I want you to leave Haran,' he said. 'Because I have a better place for you to live in.'

Now, Abraham might have said something like, 'Where?' or 'How far?' or 'Thank you very much, but I'm quite happy here.' But he didn't. In fact, he said nothing at all. He just gathered up his wife and his servants and his camels and his sheep, and went where God led him.

Why? Because Abraham trusted God. It was as simple as that.

Canaan was the name of the place where God led Abraham. And a very nice place it was. 'A land flowing with milk and honey' is what some people called it. Which means that there were many cows and goats and bees there, and plenty of flowers and grass for the animals to eat. It was altogether a pretty place. And Abraham liked it very much.

The only problem was that Abraham had no children. And besides that, both he and his wife, Sarah, were very old. Grandpa- and Grandma-old, and maybe even older than that.

But Abraham trusted God. So one night God said to him, 'Abraham, look up. Do you see the stars? One day you will have so many children and grandchildren and great-grandchildren that counting the stars will be an easy job compared with counting them.

'Now, Abraham, look down. Do you see the ground? One day, there will be more members of your family than there are bits of earth on that ground.'

What did Abraham do? He chuckled, that's what. He giggled, he chortled, he laughed! 'Me and my wife have children?' he cackled. 'We're much too old for that!'

But God wasn't joking. 'You will, indeed, have a son,' he said. 'And through your family, I will do something wonderful for the world!'

So Abraham trusted God, and it wasn't long before God sent three messengers to visit him. Abraham was very kind to them. He washed their feet, which was the polite thing to do in those days. Then he served them fresh baked bread and a creamy beef stew. It was delicious! And as the visitors were patting their tummies and wiping their mouths, they said, 'We will be back next year, and when we return, Sarah will give birth to a son!'

Someone giggled. Someone chuckled. Someone laughed. But it wasn't Abraham this time. It was Sarah, who had been listening in the tent nearby!

And, the next year, when God's promise came true and the baby was born, there was laughter again. So much laughter, in fact, that 'Laughter' is what they decided to call their son. For that is what the name 'Isaac' means.

The Bad Brother

Isaac had two sons.

The older son's name was Esau—which means 'Hairy'.

And the younger son's name was Jacob—which means something like 'Cheat'.

Isaac liked Esau the best, because he was big and strong (and hairy!), and could hunt.

One day, when Isaac was old and blind, he asked Esau to go and kill an animal, cook the meat, and bring it to him.

'When you have done that,' he promised, 'I shall tell you what you will get after I die.'

Esau ran off, his bow slung over his shoulder and his hunting knife in his hand. But he was in such a hurry that he did not notice his mother, Rebecca, hiding behind the tent.

Which son did Rebecca like best? Jacob, of course. Partly because he stayed at home to help her. And partly because he was clever and sneaky, just like her.

Rebecca decided, then and there, that Isaac's promise to Esau should go to Jacob instead. So she went and found Jacob. Together they plotted and planned. And, in no time at all, Isaac had a visitor with a steaming plate of meat.

'Back so soon, my boy? My, that meat smells delicious. Bring it here at once, Esau.'

The son brought the meat to his father. The son set it down. But the son was not Esau.

'Here you are, Father,' said Jacob in as gruff a voice as he could muster. But the old man was not fooled. Isaac may have been blind, but he was not yet deaf.

'Is that really you, Esau? Come here and let me touch those hairy arms.'

Jacob came closer. He stretched out his arms. And around them were wrapped the hairy skins from an old goat! Isaac touched the arms. He felt the hairy skin. And he smiled.

'It *is* you, Esau!' he said. 'Well then, here is my promise. When I am gone, you will have my land and grow many crops. And besides that, I am putting you in charge of the whole family. They must do whatever you tell them!'

Jacob could hardly believe it! So, when his father had kissed him, he ran off to tell his mother. And it was a good thing, for not a minute later, Esau came to his father with another plate of meat.

'I'm back!' he said cheerfully. 'And I can't wait to hear your promise.'

'What?!' exclaimed Isaac. 'I've already given my promise away!' And he told Esau what had happened.

Esau listened and, bit by bit, his face grew as red as his hair. 'Jacob!' he shouted. 'You cheat! One day I will kill you for this!'

But God was watching. And he had something very different in mind.

The Runaway

Jacob ran.

Jacob ran and ran.

Jacob had cheated his brother, Esau. And now his brother wanted to kill him. So Jacob ran.

God watched.

God watched and watched.

God watched Jacob run. And when Jacob was tired and could run no further, when Jacob fell exhausted on the desert floor with only a stone for a pillow, when Jacob was finally ready to listen, God spoke.

He came to Jacob in a dream. There was a ladder, reaching right up to heaven, with angels parading up and down. And at the very top of the ladder stood God himself!

'Jacob,' he said. 'I am the God of your father, Isaac, and your grandfather, Abraham. And I am here to make you the same promise I made to them.

'This land is yours. Your family will be great. And one day, through your family, I will do something wonderful for the whole world! Now, go and don't be afraid, for you can always count on me to protect you.'

Jacob woke up, amazed. He said 'thank you' to God and he left a stone to mark that special place.

Then Jacob ran.

He ran and ran—all the way to his Uncle Laban's house, where his mother had told him he would be safe. And where God knew he would learn an important lesson.

Now Laban had two daughters.

The older daughter's name was Leah—which means 'Tired'.

The younger daughter's name was Rachel—which means 'Lamb'.

Rachel was beautiful. And the moment Jacob set eyes on her, he knew she was the girl for him!

'Wonderful!' said his Uncle Laban. 'Work for me for seven years, and she will be your wife.'

Seven years passed, but Jacob was so in love with Rachel that it seemed no longer than a day.

The wedding was well attended. The dress was beautiful. But when Jacob pulled aside the veil that hid his bride's face, he found himself looking into Leah's tired eyes!

'Oh, I forgot to mention,' grinned Laban. 'Leah is my eldest daughter, so she has to marry first. But you can marry Rachel, next week if you like, as long as you promise to work for me for another seven years.'

Jacob looked at the ground. Now the cheater knew how it felt to be cheated.

What else could Jacob do? He waited a week, married Rachel, and worked another seven years for his Uncle Laban. Then he headed home, a very different man from the one who had run away.

Jacob walked and walked. And when his home was no more than a day's walk away, he saw Esau, his brother, walking towards him.

Jacob told his family to stay behind, and walked ahead to face his brother's anger. He wasn't running now. He believed that God would protect him.

And so God did—because Esau was different, too. When he saw Jacob, he ran up to him, reached out his hairy arms, and hugged him!

'I'm sorry,' said Jacob.

'I forgive you,' Esau answered.

And the two sons of Isaac became brothers at last.

Joseph the Dreamer

Jacob had twelve sons. That's right—twelve!

His favourite son was Joseph. Jacob spoiled him and gave him special gifts—like a beautiful coat decorated with many colours.

Reds and greens. Blues and yellows. Purples and pinks. Joseph was bright as a rainbow and proud as a peacock.

Joseph's older brothers did not like this one bit. But what they hated even more were Joseph's dreams!

'I had a dream last night,' boasted Joseph.

'Oh no,' groaned his brothers.

'I dreamed that we were all bundles of wheat. And guess what happened? Your bundles of wheat bowed down and worshipped mine!'

'And I had another dream,' Joseph bragged.

'Go on,' his brothers sighed.

'I dreamed we were all stars. And guess what? Your stars bowed down to mine, just as if I were your king!'

It didn't take long for Joseph's brothers to grow tired of this. But that's no excuse for what they did.

The next time they were out of Jacob's sight, they grabbed Joseph, tore off his

24

colourful coat, and dropped him down a dry well. They were just about to kill him, in fact, when they spotted a cloud of dust at the edge of the hill. It was a band of traders bound for Egypt, their camels loaded with goods for sale.

'Why should we kill Joseph,' asked one of the brothers, 'when we can sell him to these traders and make some money for ourselves? He'll be sold as a slave in Egypt and his foolish dreams will never come true!'

Twenty pieces of silver. That's how much the traders gave them for Joseph. And when the traders had gone, the brothers ripped up Joseph's coat, dipped it in the blood of a goat, and carried it home to their father.

'Joseph is dead,' they told Jacob. And they showed him Joseph's coat, its long sleeves shredded, its beautiful colours smeared with blood.

Jacob wept and wept.

And Joseph wept, too, as the traders carried him far from home.

Joseph the Prisoner

When the traders took Joseph to Egypt, they sold him to one of the king's own soldiers— a man named Potiphar. He was kind, and Joseph worked very hard for him. So hard, in fact, that Potiphar put Joseph in charge of all his other slaves.

Potiphar's wife, however, was evil and cruel. She told lies about Joseph and had him thrown in prison!

Things looked bad for Joseph. It seemed as if his dreams would never come true. But God was watching over him.

One morning, one of the other prisoners said, 'I had a dream last night. A strange dream. I dreamed I saw a grapevine with three branches. Suddenly, bunches of grapes burst out of those branches. So I squeezed them into a cup and gave it to the king to drink. I wonder what it means?'

Joseph listened to the dream. God listened, too. Then he whispered the dream's meaning into Joseph's ear.

'I know what it means!' said Joseph. 'Before you were sent to prison you served wine to the king. Well, in three days, you will be set free and serve him wine once more.'

That's exactly what happened. And when the wine-server was set free, he promised to help Joseph get out, too.

Two long years went by. Then, one morning, the king of Egypt said, 'I had a dream last night. A strange dream! And I can't work out what it means.'

'A dream?' said his wine-server. 'I know a man who can tell you all about your dreams.'

And straight away Joseph was brought from the prison.

'I was standing on the banks of the river,' the king told Joseph, 'when I saw seven fat cows walk up out of the water. They were chewing happily on the grass when seven other cows joined them. These cows were bony and thin, and, instead of eating the grass, they ate the first seven cows. But they stayed as skinny as ever! What can it mean?'

God whispered in Joseph's ear. Joseph listened. Then he bowed and said, 'Your Majesty, for the next seven years Egypt will grow many good crops and be as fat as those first cows. But after that, for another seven years, hardly any food at all will grow. So unless you want your people to look like those skinny cows, you must store up food in the good years and use it wisely later.'

The king was so impressed with Joseph's answer that he not only let him stay out of prison, he put him in charge of storing and saving and serving out Egypt's food.

Seven good years *were* followed by seven bad. And, after the king, Joseph became the most important man in Egypt. It was like a dream come true!

Joseph the Ruler

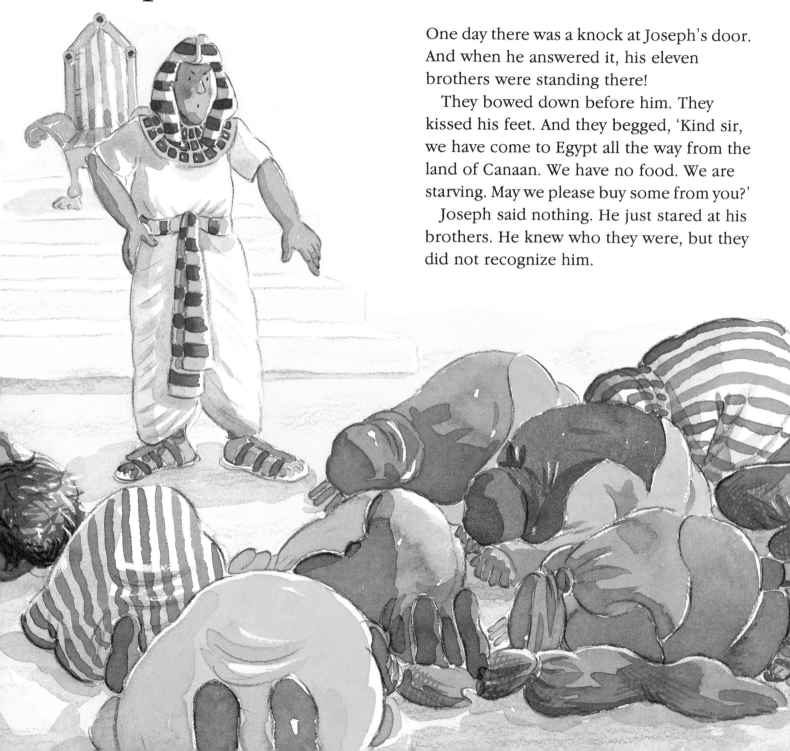

One day there was a knock at Joseph's door. And when he answered it, his eleven brothers were standing there!

They bowed down before him. They kissed his feet. And they begged, 'Kind sir, we have come to Egypt all the way from the land of Canaan. We have no food. We are starving. May we please buy some from you?'

Joseph said nothing. He just stared at his brothers. He knew who they were, but they did not recognize him.

'All right,' said Joseph, in his sternest voice. 'I will sell you food.' And he ordered his servants to load his brothers' animals.

But that wasn't all he told them to do. 'Take one of my silver cups,' he said, 'and hide it in the sack of food tied to the youngest lad's donkey.' Joseph had a plan. He wanted to see if his brothers had changed.

When Joseph's brothers reached the edge of the city, his servants stopped them and searched through their sacks. What did they find? The silver cup, of course!

'We don't know how it got there!' the brothers explained to Joseph.

'Your brother stole it, that's how,' Joseph answered. 'So he must stay here in Egypt and be my slave.'

'No, please,' begged the brothers. 'That would break our father's heart. Keep one of us, instead.'

When Joseph heard that, he knew his brothers had changed. So he told them who he was, right then and there.

'I am Joseph,' he announced, 'your long-lost brother.'

This news did not make his brothers feel any better. They were so frightened, in fact, that they could hardly speak.

'Don't be afraid,' said Joseph, 'I forgive you. You meant to hurt me, but God used what you did to save us all from this terrible famine. Now, go. Fetch my father and the rest of our family to come and live in Egypt with me.'

The brothers looked up.

The brothers grinned.

The brothers cheered!

And after a lot of hugging and hello-ing and handshaking, they set off for Canaan to tell Jacob the good news.

And Joseph? Joseph just sat back on his throne and smiled. And thanked God for making his dreams come true.

The Secret Baby

There was a basket in the water.

There was a baby in the basket!

The baby's big sister was watching from the river-bank.

And God was watching, too.

Why was the basket in the water?

Why was the baby in the basket?

Because the baby was a Hebrew—a great, great, great grandson of Abraham, Isaac, and Jacob.

'There are too many Israelites in Egypt,' the king said to his soldiers. 'If we are not careful, there will soon be more of them than of us! So I want you to kill every baby Hebrew boy.'

Some Hebrew mothers cried.

Some Hebrew mothers ran.

But this baby's mother was clever.

She covered a basket with tar—so it would not sink.

She laid her baby in the basket—and prayed that he would be quiet.

And she hid the basket in the reeds near the river-bank and hoped no one would notice.

But someone did.

And not just *any* someone. The daughter of the king himself!

She went to the river to bathe.

She spotted the basket boat.

She sent her servant to fetch it out.

And when she looked into it—oh, what a surprise!

The baby's big sister hid her eyes. She could not bear to watch.

But God kept watching. He had special plans for this baby.

'I don't care if this baby is a Hebrew,' the king's daughter announced. 'I want to keep him. Coochie-coochie-coo. I shall call him Moses. But I will need a serving woman to feed him and look after him...'

And that's when God nudged the baby's big sister, just enough so she'd jump up from where she'd been hiding.

'A serving woman?' she shouted, almost before she thought. 'I know a serving woman who can help you.'

'Well, then fetch her, girl,' commanded the princess.

And God just smiled. For now little Moses would be raised by his own mother, taught the Hebrew ways, and be ready for that day when God would use him to set his people free.

The Burning Bush

The sun was
burning hot.
Moses' skin
was burned
dark brown.
And suddenly,
he saw it—a
bright red
burning bush!
Its branches
crackled
orange and
red, and Moses
could not help but
watch—for the bush
did not burn up!
'Take off your
shoes,' came a voice from the bush. 'This is a very special place.'

'Who are you?' asked Moses. 'And why are you talking to me? I am just a poor shepherd.'

'I am the God of Abraham, Isaac, and Jacob—the God of Israel,' the voice replied. 'And you are more than a shepherd. You are Moses, the man I have chosen to lead my people out of Egypt.'

'I can't do that,' Moses trembled. 'I left Egypt years ago, and I'm an old man now.'

'You can do it. You must do it,' God answered, 'for my people are slaves in Egypt and have prayed to be set free. I have heard their prayers, and you are the man I have chosen.'

'But what if I go and they don't believe you sent me?' Moses asked.

'Take the walking stick that's in your hand,' God said, 'and throw it on the ground.'

Moses did as God told him—and the stick turned into a wriggling snake!

'Now pick it up,' God commanded.

Moses wrapped a shaking hand around the snake's scaly middle—and it turned back into a stick!

'Show them that!' God laughed. 'Then they'll believe you.'

'But I'm so shy,' Moses continued. 'I'm no good at talking to people.'

'Don't worry about that,' God assured him. 'Your brother Aaron loves to talk. You can take him with you. Now, go! My people need your help.'

So Moses went. He put on his shoes. He picked up his walking stick. And he went—off to set God's people free.

The Great Escape

Moses and Aaron went to visit the king of Egypt.

'God wants you to set his people free,' they announced.

But the king just laughed. 'Don't be silly,' he said. 'They do what I tell them. They work for nothing. I will never set them free.'

'Then I must warn you,' said Moses, 'God will make some very bad things happen until you change your mind.'

It started almost at once. The rivers of Egypt filled with blood. The houses of Egypt swarmed with frogs. The dust of Egypt turned into gnats.

But the king would not let God's people go.

The people in Egypt were covered with flies. The animals in Egypt grew sick and died. And ugly sores broke out on everyone.

But still the king would not let God's people go.

Hail pelted the land and broke down the crops. Locusts gobbled up what was left.

Then darkness like night fell for three whole days.

And still the king would not give in.

Finally, God sent an angel to kill the king's eldest son. And the eldest sons of the rest of the Egyptians.

Then, at last, the king said, 'Go! Go, and never come back!'

God's people cheered. God's people packed. God's people waved goodbye. But just as they reached the sea and were puzzling out how to get across, the king changed his mind!

He leaped into his chariot and led his army out after them. Soon, the sea stretched out before God's people and the Egyptian army rushed behind them like a wave. What could they do?

'Raise your special walking stick,' God whispered to Moses. And the sea split in two before them—leaving a path right down the middle! The people of Israel hurried along that path to the other side, the Egyptian army close behind. Just as the last of God's people had safely crossed, Moses lowered his stick, the waters rushed back, and the army was washed away.

God's people were free at last!

A Long Journey

'We're hot,' the people complained.

'We're hungry,' they moaned.

'Where are we going, anyway?' they wondered.

Moses just sighed and shook his head.

God had set the Hebrews free. And now he was leading them back to their own special land—the land he had given to Abraham, Isaac, and Jacob.

They should have been grateful. They should have been glad.

But all they could do was moan.

'We're tired.'

'We're thirsty.'

'Are we there yet?'

So Moses prayed to God. And God answered.

He made fresh water spill out of dry rocks!

He sent plump meaty quail at dinner-time.

And, for breakfast, he covered the ground with sweet white flakes. (The people called this 'manna'—a word that means, 'This tastes good—whatever it is!')

Did the Hebrews stop complaining? Not for one minute.

'We're lost.'

'We're scared.'

'We should have stayed in Egypt.'

'Don't be ridiculous!' said Moses. 'God has promised to take us to our own special land. And he has chosen us to be his own special people. We can trust him to do the very best for us.'

And so God did.

By day, he led them with a thick white cloud. By night, a flaming torch. And he showed his people the way through the wilderness.

Then God called Moses to the top of a mountain, and gave him ten important rules that showed his people how to live a good and happy life.

And finally, God showed them plans for a tabernacle—a tent where they could worship him and praise his name.

But the Hebrews followed other gods. They did not obey God's rules. And when they finally arrived at the land he had promised them, they refused to cross the border.

'We're puny.'

'We're weak.'

'We're afraid to go there,' they moaned.

So God sent them back into the wilderness. And told them that they must wander there until their children were grown.

Forty years passed. The children grew up. They were tired of wandering through the desert. And when they reached the banks of the Jordan River, there was not a moan to be heard. All they could do was cheer.

'We've arrived!'

'We're here!'

'We're home at last!'

And God's people crossed over to the Promised Land.

The Fall of Jericho

The walls of Jericho went round and round. Round and round the whole city. The walls were tall. The walls were thick. How would God's people ever get in?

Joshua's thoughts went round and round. Round and round inside his head. He was the leader of God's people now that Moses was dead. But how could he lead them into Jericho?

The sword of the Lord swung round and round. Round and round the angel's head. 'God will lead you into Jericho,' said the angel to Joshua. 'He has a secret plan. All you have to do is trust him.'

The soldiers of Israel gathered round and round. Round and round their leader, Joshua. He told them the angel's plan. He didn't leave out one bit. The soldiers were amazed!

So the army of Israel marched round and round. Round and round the walls of Jericho. Once round each day. Six days in a row. And the people of Jericho laughed.

'Why are they marching round and round? Round and round the walls of Jericho? Is this a parade? Is it some kind of trick? They'll never beat us this way!'

But when the army marched round and round, round and round on the seventh day—they marched round once, they marched round twice. They marched round Jericho seven times. Then they raised their voices. They blew their trumpets. And the walls came crashing down!

The people of Israel danced round and round. Round and round the ruins of Jericho. 'God is our helper!' they sang and they shouted. 'He will never let us down!'

A Brave and Mighty Man

'Gideon,' God whispered. 'Oh, Gideon,' God called, 'I need your help, you brave and mighty man.'

But Gideon was nowhere to be found. As a matter of fact, he was hiding—in a pit his father used for crushing grapes.

'You can't be talking to me,' Gideon stammered. 'I'm no brave and mighty man.'

But God knew what he was doing. He always does.

' You're the man all right,' God explained. 'The Midianites have my people surrounded and I want you to round up an army to stop them!'

Gideon did what God told him. And, to his surprise, over thirty thousand men agreed to join him!

'Gideon,' God whispered. 'Oh, Gideon,' God called. 'You have far too many men. I want you to send some of them away.'

'There are more Midianites than I can count!' Gideon stammered. 'I need all the help I can get.'

But God knew what he was doing. He always does.

'I am all the help you need,' God said. 'So tell the men who are frightened to go home.'

Gideon did what God told him. And when he had finished, there were only ten thousand left.

'Gideon,' God whispered. 'Oh, Gideon,' God called. 'You still have too many men. So here's what I want you to do...'

Gideon listened to God's plan. Gideon stammered and shook. Then he led his men to the river and told them to have a drink.

Some soldiers lapped up the water like dogs; Gideon sent them home.

Others got down on their knees and scooped up the water in their hands. Those were the soldiers Gideon kept. And when he had finished, there were only three hundred left!

'Gideon,' God whispered. 'Oh, Gideon,' God called. 'Now we are ready to fight the Midianites.'

'But there are thousands of them,' Gideon stammered. 'And only three hundred of us. How can we possibly win?'

'You can't,' God said. 'Not without my help. And that's what I want you to see. Now, listen. Here's my plan...'

Later that night, Gideon led his three hundred men to the edge of the Midianite camp. In one hand every soldier carried a trumpet and in the other hand an earthenware pot with a flaming torch inside. There wasn't a sword in sight! At Gideon's signal, the soldiers blew their trumpets, smashed their pots and shouted, 'For the Lord and for Gideon!'

The Midianite soldiers awoke, startled.

It seemed as if there was noise and fire all around them! Dazed and confused, they stumbled about in the dark—into each other and over each other. And it wasn't long before they were fighting each other, too!

When all the fighting had stopped, the Midianite soldiers who were left ran away, convinced that they had been defeated by some great army. But it was only Gideon, his three hundred men, and a God who knew what he was doing all along.

Samuel Hears a Voice

Now that God's people were living in their own land, there were so many things he wanted to tell them:

How to be happy.

How to take care of each other.

How to protect themselves from their enemies.

So God decided to choose someone to speak for him.

Someone he could talk to, who would then go and talk to the people. Someone called a prophet.

God looked and looked all over the land of Israel, eager to pick just the right person. And finally, he found him.

In the village of Shiloh.

In the house of Eli, the priest.

A little boy!

'Samuel,' God called, one night. 'Samuel, I want to talk with you.'

Samuel sat up and rubbed his sleepy eyes. He'd never heard God's voice before and he thought that old Eli was calling him.

Samuel stumbled into Eli's room to see what he wanted. But Eli just shooed him back to bed.

'Samuel,' God called again, 'Samuel, listen.'

Samuel was confused this time. And a little scared. So he crept back into Eli's room.

'I told you, boy,' yawned the old priest. 'I didn't call you. Now off to bed!'

Samuel didn't know what to think as he crawled under his covers. But when God called, 'Samuel, Samuel,' for the third time, he knew what to do.

He dashed back to Eli, just as fast as he could!

'Samuel,' sighed Eli, 'if either of us is going to get any sleep tonight, we need to find out who's calling you. And I have an idea who it might be. So, the next time you hear that voice, I don't want you to come running in here. Instead, I want you to say, "Speak, Lord, and I will listen." '

Samuel's eyes opened wide.

'You mean it's God who's calling me?'

'Do as I tell you,' said Eli, 'and we'll find out.'

So Samuel went back to bed.

God called his name again.

This time Samuel stayed there and listened to God, and his eyes opened wide with wonder.

And from that moment until Samuel was himself an old man, God talked to Samuel, giving him messages to pass on to the people. And, just like the first time, God's messages never failed to leave him wide-eyed with wonder.

David the Giant-Killer

Goliath was big.

He had to stoop to get through doorways. His head was always bumping up against the ceiling. And his friends thought twice before inviting him to dinner.

Goliath had a big spear. Ten feet long, at least. With a big iron point. And his big bronze armour weighed a hundred pounds or more.

Goliath had a big voice, too.

And, one day, he used it. He stamped out in front of his army and shouted across the valley to the soldiers camped on the other side.

'I am Goliath!' he bellowed. 'And I dare any of you to come and fight me. Win the fight, and we will be your slaves. Lose, and you must work for us.'

David was little.

Just a boy, really, who looked after the sheep. When he wanted a break from that, he carried cheese to his brothers in the army. And that's what he was doing one day, when he heard Goliath shout.

David was a little angry.

'Who does that giant think he is?' huffed David. 'Doesn't he know that the Lord God himself watches over us? Why, with God's help, even I could beat that bully.'

So David took a little walk. He went to see the king.

'I want to fight the giant,' he announced.

And the king almost fell off his throne.

'But you are so little,' said the king. 'And he is so big!'

'A lion is big,' answered David. 'And so is a bear. But when they came after my sheep, the Lord God helped me face them and fight them off. He will do the same with this giant.'

'All right,' the king agreed. 'But at least let me lend you my armour.'

The armour was big. Too big. And so heavy that David could hardly move.

So he gave it back. And picked up five little stones instead. And a sling. And his trusty shepherd's staff.

Goliath gave a big laugh when he saw the little shepherd boy.

And he took two big steps.

David ran a little way.

Two more giant steps for Goliath.

And David ran a little further.

They were in the middle of the valley now, and everything was quiet.

Goliath roared a big roar, sucked in a big breath of air, and raised his big spear.

David sneaked his little hand into his little pouch, pulled out a little stone, and slipped it in his sling. Then he spun it round his head and let it fly.

And before the giant could say another word, the stone struck him on the head, and he fell with a big thud to the ground.

David's side shouted a big 'Hooray!'

Goliath's side whispered, 'Uh-oh.'

And from then on, some pretty big things happened to the little shepherd boy. He was given a king's reward. He was promised the hand of the king's daughter. And, one day, he became king himself! The very best king God's people ever had.

The Wise King

When David died, his son Solomon became Israel's new king. And what do you think was the very first thing he did?

Pass some new law? No.

Send his army to fight some new enemy? Not likely.

Order himself a fancy new crown? Never.

No, the first thing he did was to kneel down before God and pray.

'Good for you!' God said to Solomon. 'Now what would you like me to give you?'

Solomon could have prayed for anything. Anything at all! But what do you think he asked for?

A long life? No.

Victory in battle? Not likely.

Loads of money? Never.

No, the only thing he asked for was . . . wisdom!

'It's going to be hard ruling over all these people,' he prayed. 'And I want to do the best job that I can. So help me, God. Give me wisdom to make the right choices and do the right things.'

Well, God was so pleased with Solomon's choice that he promised to give him wisdom—*and* all the other things, as well. A long life, victory, and loads of money!

It wasn't long before Solomon's wisdom was put to the test.

Two women came to see him one day. One of them was holding a baby. And the other one was very unhappy.

'That women stole my baby!' she cried. 'Her baby died. And while I was sleeping, she came and took mine!'

'That's a lie!' shouted the woman with the baby. And she held the child even more tightly.

Solomon looked at the women. Solomon looked at the baby. And what do you think he did?

Give the baby to the first woman? No.

Give the baby to the second woman? Not likely.

Keep it for himself? Never.

No, he called one of his soldiers and told him to raise his sword above the child.

'Now cut the baby in half,' Solomon ordered, 'and each of the women can have a piece.'

The soldier was shocked. He looked at the king. He looked at the baby. But before he could use his sword, the woman who claimed her child had been stolen cried, 'Stop! Let her have the child. He's my baby, but I'd rather see him raised by another than have him cut in two.'

'Oh no,' said the woman holding the baby.

'The king is right. Cut the baby in half!'

It was exactly what Solomon had hoped for.

'Now I see who the real mother is,' he said. 'She would rather give up her child than see it harmed.' And he took the baby from one woman and gave it to the other.

And what do you think God's people did?

They clapped.

They cheered.

And they thanked God for giving them a king who was both wise and good.

God Sends Fire

If David was the best king God's people ever had, then Ahab was one of the worst!

He didn't listen to the Lord God at all.

No, he worshipped a statue called Baal. And, what is worse, he made a lot of God's people do the same.

God was watching this, of course. And he was not happy that his people had forgotten him and had replaced him with a god who was nothing more than a pile of stones.

So he whispered into the ear of Elijah, a man who had not forgotten him.

'Elijah,' God whispered, 'tell King Ahab that what he is doing is wrong. Tell him that I will stop the rain from falling until he stops worshipping Baal.'

Elijah swallowed hard and passed God's message on to Ahab. But Ahab only laughed. That is, until it stopped raining.

One year went by.

Another year followed.

And there was not one drop of rain.

So, in the third year, Elijah went to see King Ahab again.

'Elijah, you trouble-maker!' Ahab roared. 'See what you have done! The crops have died. The wells are dry. And it's *all* your fault!'

'No, Your Majesty,' said Elijah. 'The fault is yours, for you have not obeyed the Lord God.'

'The Lord God—ha!' snapped Ahab. 'I don't have to listen to what he says. I follow Baal.'

'All right, then,' answered Elijah. 'Why don't we have a contest—to prove once and for all who the true God really is?'

And so they did—on the top of Mount Carmel, overlooking the sea. Elijah, prophet of the Lord God, stood on one side. Four hundred and fifty prophets of Baal stood on the other. And the people of Israel gathered around the bottom to watch.

The prophets of Baal went first. They stacked up a pile of wood. They killed a bull and laid it on the top. Then they prayed to Baal, and asked him to set the whole thing on fire. They prayed hard. They prayed long—from breakfast to lunchtime. But there was no fire. Not even a spark.

Elijah couldn't resist having a little fun. 'Perhaps Baal is asleep,' he joked. 'Or day-dreaming, or on holiday! Or maybe he's just a little hard of hearing.'

And so Baal's prophets prayed louder. But it made no difference, and by the middle of the afternoon they were exhausted.

And that's when Elijah took his turn. He piled up twelve stones—one for each of the sons of Jacob. He laid wood on top of that, then the bull. Finally he poured water over the whole thing!

The crowd was amazed. How would it ever catch fire?

But Elijah knew just what he was doing. 'Lord,' he prayed, 'you are the real God. Please show that to your people now, so they will follow you again.'

Elijah had barely opened his eyes when it happened. God sent fire from heaven that burned up not only the bull, but the water, stones and wood, as well!

'The Lord is God!' the people shouted.

Then they cheered for Elijah, chased away the prophets of Baal, and ran for cover. Because, suddenly, it had started to rain!

The Helpful Servant

Naaman was a soldier. Not just any soldier, but the commander of the whole Syrian army! He was a very powerful man. But he was afraid.

Naaman, you see, was ill, and no one knew how to make him well. His skin was covered with sores, and he couldn't feel his fingers or his feet. Everyone felt sorry for him. And God felt sorry, too.

So God whispered to a little girl who had been captured by Naaman's army and carried away from God's promised land. She worked for Naaman's wife, and one day she said to her mistress, 'Back in Israel, where I come from, there lives a man called Elisha. God uses him to make sick people well. If only Naaman could go and see him.'

And before long the great soldier, who had fought against God's people, was off to seek help from God's prophet.

Naaman didn't go alone. He took his servants. And his horses. And a chariot full of treasure—to reward Elisha in case his cure should work.

It was a grand parade, and Naaman expected a grand greeting in return. But when he sent one of his men to knock on Elisha's door, the prophet did not even answer. Instead he told his servant Gehazi to say: 'If you want to be well, go and dip yourself seven times in the Jordan River.'

Now it may be that Naaman was tired and frustrated. Or it may simply be that he was proud. Whatever the reason, the prophet's message made him angry.

'The Jordan River?' he shouted. 'It's filthy! I'll throw myself into any river back in Syria. But I will not stick one toe in the Jordan, or take the advice of a man who cannot even be bothered to meet me!'

'Begging your pardon, sir,' mumbled one of Naaman's servants, 'but if the prophet had sent you off to do something hard, you would have gone straight away, wouldn't you?'

'Of course,' grunted Naaman. 'Any soldier would!'

'Well then, why can't you go and do something easy—like washing in the river? It can't hurt, and it just might work!'

Naaman sighed, 'All right.' And led his men to the river.

He dipped himself twice. Nothing.

He dunked himself twice more. His skin was as ugly as ever.

Twice more, and still no cure. Naaman was getting angry again.

But when he came up for the seventh time, spluttering and shaking the water from his face, Naaman's men let out a cheer. Naaman opened his eyes and looked at his hands. The sores were gone! Gone from all over his body.

Naaman dressed and hurried back to Elisha's house. The prophet himself answered the door this time, and Naaman could not contain his joy.

'Take this treasure. Take it all!' Naaman begged. 'For you have saved my life.'

But Elisha said no, for it was God, after all, who had healed Naaman.

'All right, then,' said Naaman, scooping up a pile of earth, 'let me take this with me, so that I can stand on a piece of your land and worship your God, too.'

Elisha nodded and smiled.

And God smiled, too. For, with a little girl and a muddy river, he had turned an enemy into a friend.

Jonah the Groaner

Jonah was a groaner.

That's right—a groaner.

So when God told him to go to Nineveh and tell the people who lived there to change their evil ways, what did Jonah do?

Jonah groaned.

'Not Nineveh!' he groaned. 'Anywhere but Nineveh. The people who live there are our enemies!'

And when he had stopped groaning, Jonah bought himself a ticket. A ticket for a boat ride. A boat ride that would take him far away from Nineveh.

God listened to Jonah groan. God watched him buy his ticket. But God still wanted Jonah to go to Nineveh.

So when the boat reached the deepest part of the sea, God sent a storm.

'God, help us!' cried a sailor. 'We're sinking!'

'God, save us!' cried another. 'We're tipping over!'

'God must be very angry,' cried the captain, 'with someone here on board.'

And what did Jonah do? Jonah groaned.

'It's me,' Jonah groaned. 'I'm the one God's angry with. He told me to go to Nineveh, and here I am, sailing in the opposite direction. Throw me into the sea and your troubles will be over.'

'God, forgive us!' the sailors cried as they tossed Jonah into the water. And almost at once, the sea grew calm.

'Oh dear,' Jonah groaned, 'I'm sinking.'

'Oh no,' Jonah groaned, 'I'm going to drown.'

'Oh my,' Jonah groaned, 'that's the biggest fish I've ever seen!'

And before he could groan another groan, the fish opened its mouth and swallowed Jonah up!

It was God who sent the fish—to rescue Jonah, and to give him time to think. He had plenty to groan about, of course—the fish's slimy stomach, the seaweed, the smell. But Jonah was still alive—and that was something to cheer about! So Jonah stopped his groaning and prayed a prayer:

'I was sinking, Lord. I was drowning. But you saved me. So now I will do whatever you want.'

Three days later, the fish spat Jonah up on a beach. And Jonah kept his promise—he went straight to Nineveh and told the people that God wanted them to change their evil ways.

'Forty days is all you've got,' he warned them. 'And if you haven't changed by then, God will destroy your city.'

The people of Nineveh listened. The people of Nineveh wept. Then the people of Nineveh changed! From the king right down to the poorest slave, they decided to do what was right.

And what did Jonah do? Jonah groaned. He sat himself down in the shadow of a tree, and he groaned.

'I knew this would happen,' he groaned. 'You are a loving God who loves to forgive. But I still don't like the people of Nineveh and I wish they had been destroyed.'

Jonah fell asleep, groaning. And during the night, God sent a worm to kill the tree. When Jonah awoke, he groaned more than ever.

'The tree is dead!' he groaned. 'And now I have no shade.'

'Oh, Jonah,' God sighed. 'You cry about this tree, but you care nothing for the people of Nineveh. I want you to love them like I do.'

'And finally,' God added, 'I want you to stop your groaning!'

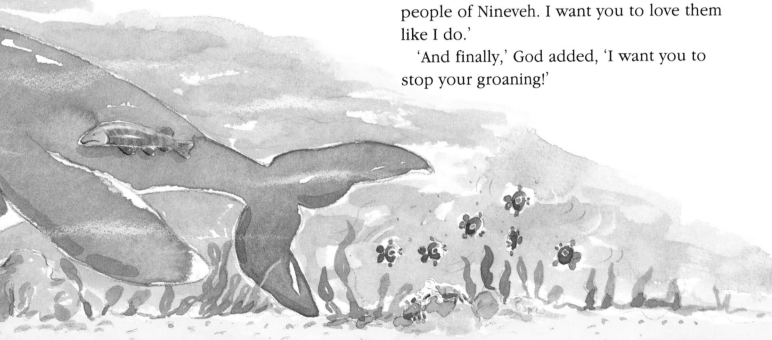

Down in the Well

Down in the well. Deep down in the well. Deep down in the very bottom of the well, there was no water!

But down in the well. Deep down in the well. Deep down in the very bottom of the well, there were spiders and slugs and slithering snakes—and the prophet Jeremiah.

What was he doing down in the well? Deep down in the very bottom of the well?

He was waiting, that's what, and wondering and wishing for someone to pull him out.

God had whispered in the prophet's ear, you see. And Jeremiah had passed the message on to the king.

'Change your ways! Do what's right! Or I will let your enemies, the Babylonians, conquer your country and turn your people into slaves.'

The king did not want to hear this message. And he didn't want anyone else to hear it, either.

So he had God's messenger, poor Jeremiah, dropped down in the well. Deep down in the well. Deep down in the very bottom of the well.

It was dark down there. Too dark for Jeremiah to see. But it wasn't too dark for God! He saw Jeremiah brush a spider off his face. He watched as the snakes slithered closer.

And then God did something. He whispered into the ear of one of the king's servants, a man called Ebed-Melech. And he told him to go and fetch his dirty laundry!

Down in the well. Deep down in the well. Deep down to the very bottom of the well dropped Ebed-Melech's laundry. And it landed right on Jeremiah's head.

'Hey!' hollered the prophet. 'What's this?'

'My clothes!' called Ebed-Melech. 'Everything but what I'm wearing on my back. I've tied them together like a rope. Now wrap them around you, quickly, and I will pull you out.'

And so, more determined than ever to pass on God's message, the prophet rose up from the well. Right up from the well. Right up from the very bottom of the well.

Daniel and the Lions

God was very sad. Most of his people had stopped listening to him, and talking to him, and following his rules.

'If you do not change your ways,' he warned them, 'you will have to leave this special country I gave you long ago.'

But the people would not listen. So God let their enemies defeat them, and destroy their cities, and carry them hundreds of miles away to be slaves in another land.

There were, however, a few of God's people who did not forget him. One of them was Daniel.

He worked hard in the new land—so hard that he became one of the king's own helpers! But he never forgot about God, or failed to pray to him, morning, noon and night.

Some of the king's men were jealous of Daniel. They wanted his job for themselves. So they talked the king into making a new law, a law which said, 'No one, but no one, is allowed to pray to anyone but the king himself.'

'We've got Daniel, now!' his enemies laughed.

And so they had. For the very next morning, Daniel knelt by his window, bowed his head and prayed—not to the king, but to God.

'Thank you for taking care of us in this faraway land,' he prayed. 'Forgive us, and please take us back to our own land, soon.'

Daniel's enemies were watching. And before he could even open his eyes, they grabbed him and dragged him in front of the king.

The king was sad. Very sad. He liked Daniel. But he could not break his own law.

'Daniel must be punished,' he sighed. 'Throw him into the lion pit.'

But even as the king gave the order, he whispered a prayer that no one could hear. A prayer to Daniel's God that, somehow, Daniel might be saved.

The pit was dark. The pit was deep. The lions covered its floor like a shaggy growling carpet. They leaped to their feet in a second when Daniel landed among them. They licked their lips. They showed their teeth. Their eyes shone bright and fierce. They opened their mouths and moved towards their dinner. And then they stopped.

'Shoo! Scat! Go away!' shouted a voice right behind Daniel.

The lions' mouths snapped shut. Their tails drooped. And they whimpered away to the corners of the cave.

Slowly Daniel turned around, and looked up into the face of an enormous angel!

'Nothing to worry about, now,' the angel smiled. 'God sent me to watch over you. Why don't you get some sleep?'

The next morning, the king cheered when he discovered that Daniel was still alive.

'Pull Daniel out,' he ordered his men. 'And while you're at it, take the men that talked me into that silly law and dump them into the pit instead.'

The king put his arm around Daniel and walked him back to the palace.

Meanwhile Daniel's enemies cried for help. And the lions enjoyed their breakfast!

A Time to Build

'My people have learned their lesson,' God decided. 'It's time for them to come home.'

So God whispered in the ear of Cyrus, king of the country where God's people were slaves. 'Send them home,' God said.

So Cyrus did. And thousands and thousands of people returned to Jerusalem.

There was a lot of work to do when they got there: rebuilding their houses—so they had somewhere to live; rebuilding the temple—so they had somewhere to worship God; rebuilding the walls around Jerusalem—so they had somewhere to hide from their enemies.

It was hard work. They had no end of problems. And for a long time it looked as if it would never be done.

And then Cyrus died. And another king took his place. And God took the chance to help his people by whispering in the ear of a man who could get *that* king's attention.

The man's name was Nehemiah. His job was to bring the king his wine each day—and to taste it first, to see that no one had put any poison in it! The king trusted him very much, and was puzzled when Nehemiah arrived one day, cup in hand, with a sad frown on his face.

'What's the matter, Nehemiah?' the king asked. 'Why do you look so sad?'

Nehemiah whispered a prayer before he answered.

'Forgive me, Your Majesty,' Nehemiah begged. 'I know it is my duty to smile in your presence, but I cannot. I have heard that my people are suffering in their homeland. The walls of Jerusalem are broken down and I know that I could help, if only I could go and join them.

'I know also that you have wood and stone which would make their job so much easier. Please, send me there with supplies to finish the job and bring an end to my people's suffering.'

The king thought long and hard. 'Yes, Nehemiah,' he answered. 'You may go. But let me send some of my soldiers along, to protect you on the way.'

Nehemiah thanked the king.
He thanked God, too.
And he set off on
his long journey.

When Nehemiah arrived, he found Jerusalem in a terrible state. But the people were pleased to see him.

'Let's build up these walls,' he encouraged them. 'For God is with us. He gave me courage to speak to the king. He persuaded the king to give us these supplies. And now God will help us finish the job.'

The people cheered and set to work. It still wasn't easy. There were enemies to deal with, so sometimes they had to work with a hammer in one hand and a sword in the other. But finally they finished. The walls were built. Their houses too. And they had even finished the temple, where the people gathered to talk with God.

'Forgive us for not listening to you,' they prayed. 'We promise to do better in the future—to live the way you told us when you gave us this land so long ago. Thank you for giving us another chance, and for bringing us home at last!'

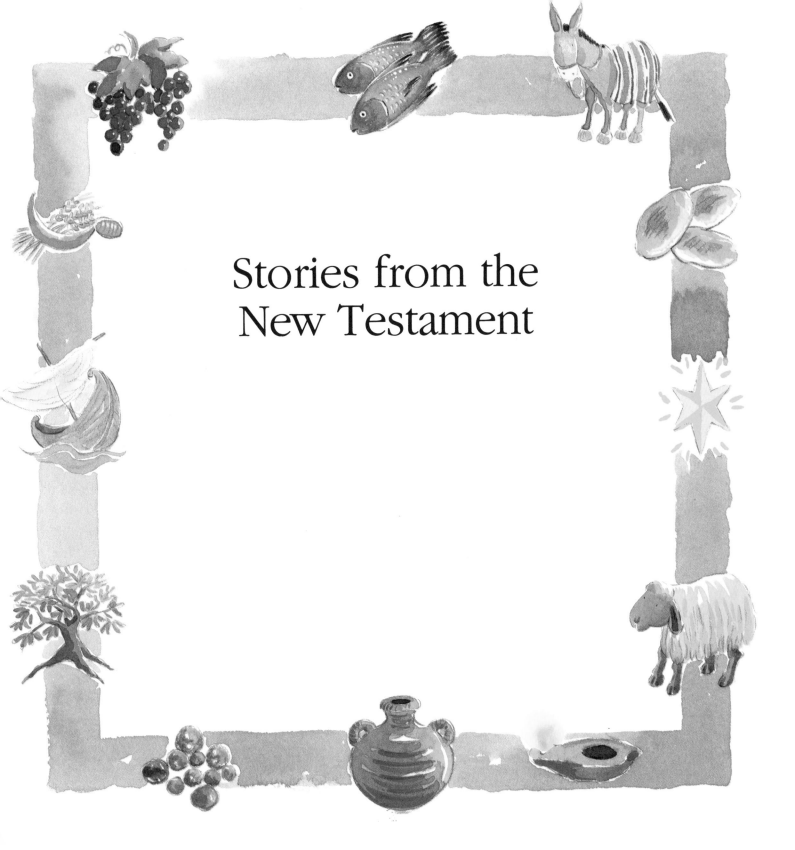

Stories from the
New Testament

The First Christmas

'Good news!' said the angel to a girl named Mary. 'God is sending Someone Special into the world. He will be a great king. His name will be Jesus. And guess what? God wants you to be his mother!'

'Good news!' said the angel to a carpenter named Joseph. 'God is sending Someone Special into the world. He will rescue everyone from the wrong things they have done. He will be God's own Son! But guess what? God wants you to take his mother Mary as your wife, and raise little Jesus as your own.'

'Bad news!' sighed Joseph to Mary. 'The rulers of our country want to count us, to see how many of us there are. And to make it easier for them, we have to go back to our home town. That means a trip all the way from Nazareth to Bethlehem! And with the baby due so soon . . .'

'Bad news!' sighed the innkeeper, shaking his head. 'There's not one room left in Bethlehem. But seeing as the young lady's expecting and all, why don't you spend the night in my stable?'

'Good news!' smiled Joseph, handing the baby to Mary. 'It's a boy, just as God promised. God's own Son, there in your arms—Jesus.'

'Good news!' called the angel to the shepherds on the hill. 'God has sent Someone Special into the world. The someone you have been waiting for. If you hurry into Bethlehem, you can see him for yourselves. He's just a baby now, wrapped up warmly and lying in a manger. But one day he will save you from all that is wrong. One day he will bring you peace!'

Then the angels filled the sky with a good news song. The shepherds went to Bethlehem and made a good news visit. And, on that very first Christmas Day, Mary just watched, and rocked her baby, and smiled a good news smile!

The Wise Men's Visit

The sky was black. The night was clear. The stars were bright as diamonds.

'Perfect,' said the star-watcher. 'Just as it should be.' But just then God nudged the brightest star and sent it floating like a kite across the night sky.

'Quick,' called the star-watcher to his friends. 'Come and see. There's a new star and that means...'

'... a new king!' said the second star-watcher. 'Somewhere a new king is about to be born!'

'I'll tell you what,' said the third star-watcher, 'let's follow the star and see.'

So the three star-watchers climbed onto their camels and set off after the star. When it zigged, they zigged. When it zagged, they zagged—across deserts and mountains and rivers. Until they reached the land of God's people, the Jews.

'We have come a long way,' explained the first star-watcher to King Herod.

'We have followed a remarkable star,' explained the second star-watcher.

'So can you tell us where the baby is?' asked the third star-watcher. 'The baby born King of the Jews?'

'King of the Jews? King of the Jews?' King Herod repeated, trying hard not to look upset. 'Let me speak with my advisers.'

And so King Herod called a meeting. A meeting that was not very happy.

'King of the Jews?' the king shouted. 'King of the Jews? I AM THE KING OF THE JEWS!!'

'Y-yes, Your Majesty,' his advisers mumbled. 'But God has always promised that one day he would send us a special king. P-perhaps he is the one the star-watchers are looking for.'

'Hmm,' Herod muttered. 'And where does God say this special king will be born?'

'In Bethlehem, Your Majesty. The city of David.'

'Send for the star-watchers,' King Herod ordered. 'I have decided what I shall do.'

'Gentlemen,' said the king, 'the child you seek is somewhere in Bethlehem. Go to him. Find him. Then come and tell me where he is, so that I can visit him, too.'

The king said this with a smile, but his heart was black, black as a night without stars. And he had already determined to kill the child, so no one would take his place as king.

The star-watchers didn't know that when they left, but they soon found out. For the same God who had nudged the star visited them in a dream and told them the king's dark plan.

So they went to see young Jesus, and gave him gifts of gold and frankincense and myrrh. And then they went straight home, with stars in their eyes and God in their hearts.

65

The Boy in the Temple

'Excuse me,' said Mary, 'but have you seen my boy, Jesus?'

'I'm sorry to trouble you,' said Joseph, 'but I can't seem to find my son. He's twelve and about so tall.'

Again and again they asked, but Mary and Joseph found nothing but shrugs and sympathetic looks and 'Sorry, I can't help you.'

They were worried. They were scared. They didn't know what else to do. And what made it worse was that this should have been such a wonderful trip—off to Jerusalem to visit the temple and celebrate the Passover holiday. But now they were on their way home—and Jesus was missing!

It was getting dark. 'We've asked everyone we came with,' Mary wept. 'And no one has seen him.'

Joseph snapped his fingers. 'What about those boys? The ones from the next village? Jesus walked with them awhile on the way down here.'

'I've already spoken to them,' sighed Mary, wiping her eyes. 'Nothing.'

'Then there's only one thing left to do,' said Joseph. 'We must go back to Jerusalem and look for him there.'

And so they went, retracing their steps—road by road, street by street, alley by alley, until they arrived, exhausted, at the temple.

'Have you seen a boy?' said Joseph to one of the temple priests. 'He's twelve, he's . . .'

'Have we seen a boy?' the priest grinned. 'We certainly have. His name is Jesus, right?'

'Yes!' cried Joseph. 'But how did you know?'

'Come with me,' the priest chuckled, 'and I'll show you.'

The priest led them to a corner of the temple courtyard. There was a crowd gathered, listening to one of the temple teachers. And seated right at the teacher's feet was Jesus!

'The boy is remarkable!' the priest

whispered to Joseph. 'He has been going from teacher to teacher, asking the most amazing questions. And when the teachers quiz him, he answers with a wisdom well beyond his years. You should be very proud!'

'I'm certainly amazed,' Joseph sighed. 'But I would be much prouder if he hadn't worried his mother and me half to death. We should be halfway back to Nazareth by now!'

When the teacher had finished, Joseph and Mary rushed straight to Jesus. They hugged him, they led him out of the temple, but it didn't take long before they told him how they felt.

'What did you think you were doing?' Mary asked. 'We were worried sick!'

'I'm sorry,' Jesus said. 'I thought you'd know where I was.' Then he looked back at the temple and whispered, 'It is my Father's house, after all.'

Mary and Joseph looked at each other. Jesus took their hands. And together they started off home.

Jesus is Baptized

John was shouting.

John was shouting in the wilderness.

'God is sending Someone Special!' he shouted. 'And you'd better get ready to meet him.'

Many people listened to John. They thought that he was someone special. He lived in the wilderness, after all, by the River Jordan. He wore a scratchy camel-hair shirt. And he ate locusts for lunch!

'I'm not the Special One,' John shouted. 'Why, I'm not even special enough to stoop down and undo his sandals. No, I'm just here to help you get ready to meet him.'

'And how do we do that?' someone shouted back.

'You repent!' John shouted. 'That's how! You stop doing what's bad and you start doing what's good. If you meet a poor man, you don't tell him to go away—you give him food and clothes. If you're a tax collector, you don't take more than you're supposed to—you're honest and kind. And if you're a soldier, you don't bully people—you protect them and take care of them.'

'And what about us?' shouted some Very Religious People.

'You,' John shouted, louder than ever, 'need to stop pretending that you're perfect—and admit that you have done things that make God sad! I'll say it again— God is sending Someone Special! And you—all of you—need to get ready to meet him. So come, let me dip you in this river to show God that you want your lives to change.'

The people came. John dipped them in the river. And then, one day, when all the shouting and dipping was done, someone else came, too.

It was Jesus. Thirty years old now and all grown up. John recognized him right away, and stopped his shouting. 'You're the Special One, aren't you?' he whispered. And Jesus just smiled.

'That's right,' Jesus said. 'And I want you to dip me, too.'

'Oh, no,' John said, 'It should be the other way around!'

'Listen,' said Jesus. 'It's time I began the work I was sent to do. And this is how my Father wants me to get started.'

So John agreed, and he and Jesus waded out into the water. John dipped Jesus in the river, and when he came back up again, shaking the wet hair from his eyes, the clouds parted and a dove landed on Jesus' shoulder. It was a sign that God was with Jesus.

'Well done, Son,' God said. 'I'm proud of you. You really are Someone Very Special.'

Jesus' Special Friends

Jesus grew up in a place called Galilee, where there was a large and beautiful lake. And it was there that he began the work God gave him to do.

'God is like a king,' he told the people. 'And he wants all of you to be a part of his kingdom—to love him and to love each other.'

People liked to hear Jesus talk. In fact, one morning, the crowd was so huge that Jesus was nearly pushed into the sea.

'Excuse me,' Jesus asked a fisherman, 'could I borrow your boat for a while?'

The fisherman's name was Peter. 'Of course,' he said. 'It's doing me no good. I was out all night and didn't catch a thing.'

Jesus climbed into the boat. Peter rowed it a little way from shore. And, from there, Jesus talked to the crowd. When he had finished, Jesus sent the people home. And then he turned to Peter.

'Let's go a little further out,' he whispered. 'I'd like to catch some fish.'

Peter tossed back his head and laughed. 'I told you. Me and my men were out all night. We caught nothing!'

Jesus didn't say a word. He just smiled and looked across the lake.

'All right,' Peter sighed. 'If that's what you want.'

So Peter sailed to the deepest part of the lake. Then he dropped his fishing nets over the side.

It took no time at all. The nets started pulling and jerking and stretching. And it was all Peter could do to keep the boat from tipping over.

'Help!' Peter called to some friends nearby. 'Help me, please!' And they rowed to him as fast as they could.

Then, all together, the men pulled on the nets—and the fish came tumbling and slapping onto the decks of both boats. Red fish and blue fish, not just one or two fish. So many, in fact, that the boats would have sunk, had the fishermen not rowed quickly back to shore.

Peter looked at the fish. Peter looked at his friends. Then Peter looked at Jesus, and fell to his knees, trembling.

'Only God, or somebody full of his power, could do that,' Peter said. 'And why would someone like that want to go fishing with the likes of me?'

Jesus shook his head and smiled. 'Don't be scared,' he said. 'God has given me a lot of work to do. And I need helpers. Helpers like you and your friends. Once you were fishermen. But from now on, you'll be fishing for people. And helping me bring them to God.'

Then Jesus stepped out of the boat and walked away, across the shore. 'Come with me,' he called.

Peter and his friends watched him go. They looked at the fish. They looked at each other. Then they dropped their nets, left their boats behind, and raced off to follow Jesus.

Down Through the Roof

Anna stuck a finger through the hole in her skirt.

'How did that get there?' she wondered.

She would have run to her mother to have it mended, but her mother was on the other side of the house. And the house was full.

Packed full.

Jammed full.

Chock-a-block full.

Why? Because Jesus was visiting.

The old man and woman standing in front of Anna shifted, and she squeezed into the hole between them. She could see better now.

Jesus was a lot like her father. They both taught people about God. They both prayed beautiful prayers. But Jesus could do something else. Something her father had never done. Jesus could make sick people well! No wonder the whole town had crowded into her house.

Suddenly something dropped on Anna's head.

Anna looked up. And there was another hole—a hole in the roof!

Anna stepped back.

The hole got bigger.

The crowd stepped back.

And the hole got bigger still.

'What's going on up there?' shouted Anna's father. And, instead of an answer, a man dropped through the hole. A man lying on a mat with a rope at each corner. A poor, sick man who could not even move. His friends lowered him carefully to the floor, and Jesus gently laid a hand on his head.

'My friend,' Jesus said, 'the wrong things you have done are now forgiven.'

'Wait a minute!' growled Anna's father. 'Wait just a minute. Only God can take away someone's sins. Just who do you think you are?'

'Oh dear,' thought Anna. Her father often got angry when he talked with people about God.

But Jesus wasn't angry at all. 'Which is easier?' he said calmly. 'To forgive a lame man's sins, or to make him walk?'

It was all Anna could do not to giggle. 'What a silly question,' she thought. 'One is just as hard as the other.'

'Well,' Jesus continued. 'To show you that God has given me the power to fix what is wrong in this man's heart, I shall fix what is wrong with his legs.'

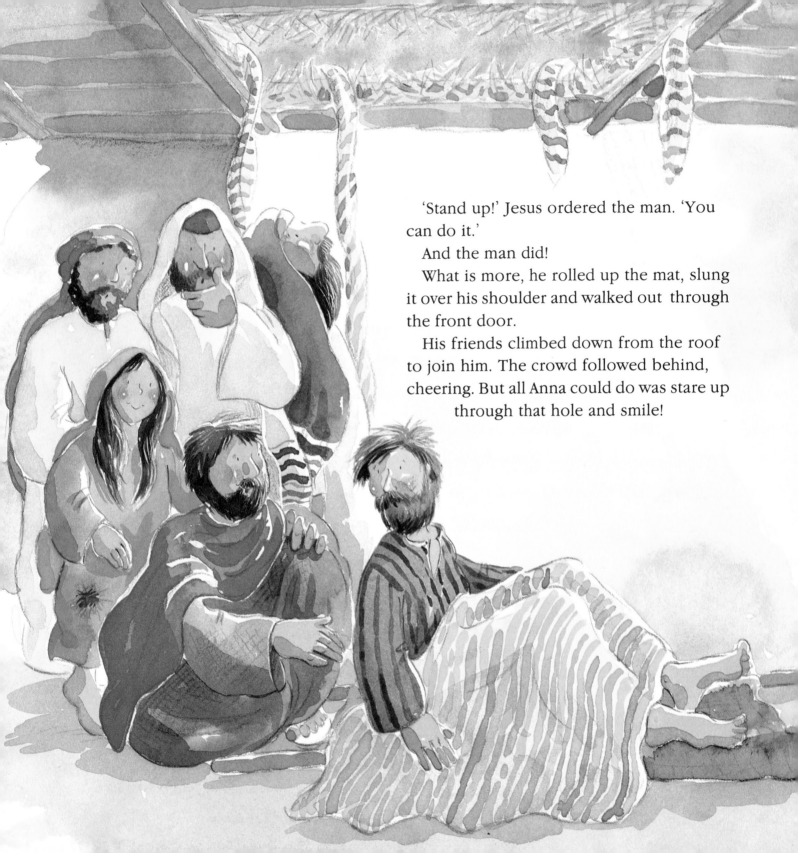

'Stand up!' Jesus ordered the man. 'You can do it.'

And the man did!

What is more, he rolled up the mat, slung it over his shoulder and walked out through the front door.

His friends climbed down from the roof to join him. The crowd followed behind, cheering. But all Anna could do was stare up through that hole and smile!

The Storm on the Lake

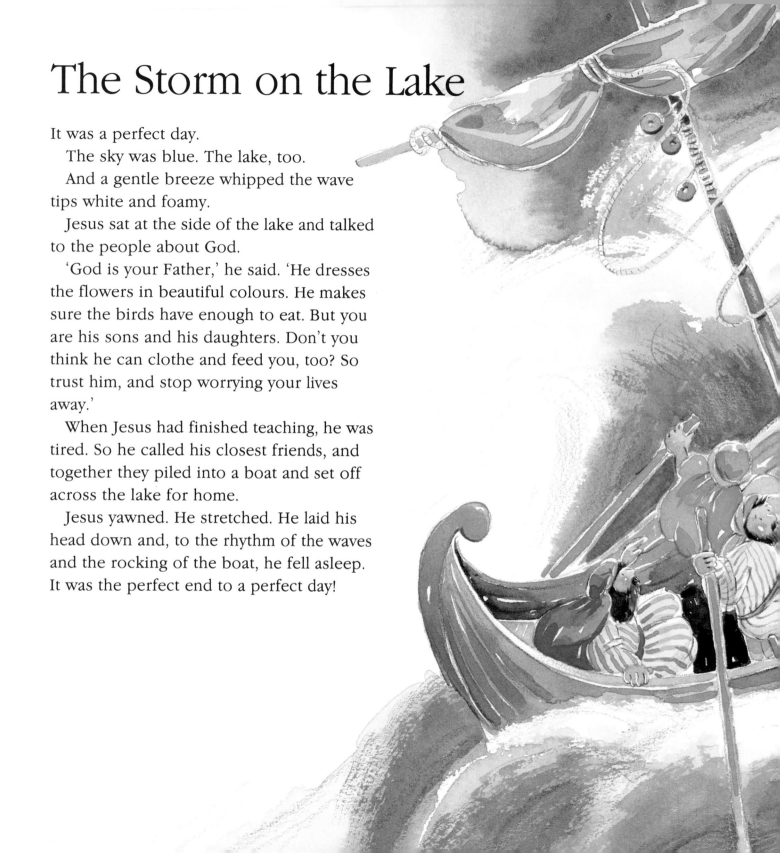

It was a perfect day.

The sky was blue. The lake, too.

And a gentle breeze whipped the wave tips white and foamy.

Jesus sat at the side of the lake and talked to the people about God.

'God is your Father,' he said. 'He dresses the flowers in beautiful colours. He makes sure the birds have enough to eat. But you are his sons and his daughters. Don't you think he can clothe and feed you, too? So trust him, and stop worrying your lives away.'

When Jesus had finished teaching, he was tired. So he called his closest friends, and together they piled into a boat and set off across the lake for home.

Jesus yawned. He stretched. He laid his head down and, to the rhythm of the waves and the rocking of the boat, he fell asleep. It was the perfect end to a perfect day!

And then, suddenly, the day was not so perfect.

The sky turned black. The lake, too.

And a wild wind stirred the waves up tall and stormy.

The boat rocked right. The boat rocked left. The boat rocked up and down. The boat rocked so hard, in fact, that Jesus' friends were sure they would all drown.

But Jesus slept right through it—except for the odd snuffle and snore.

'Jesus!' his friends called at last. 'Jesus! Wake up! We're all going to drown!'

So Jesus woke up. Then he sat up. Then he rubbed his eyes and he stood up. It was all anybody else could do to stay on their feet. But Jesus stood up! And then, very calmly, he said to the wind, 'Quiet now.' And he said to the waves, 'Settle down.'

And they did!

Then Jesus turned to his friends and said, 'You didn't need to be frightened. You didn't have to worry. All you had to do was trust me. See, everything is calm.'

And so it was. The sky was blue. The lake, too. And the little waves splashed happily at the side of the boat.

It was a perfect day, again!

'Time to Get Up'

'Jesus! Help me, Jesus! My daughter is dying!' Jairus shouted as loud as he could, and the crowd parted to let him through.

'She's only twelve,' he explained. 'And she's so ill. But I know I can count on you to make her well. Please!'

Jesus nodded. 'Show me the way,' he said. But the minute they started wading through the crowd, Jesus stopped.

'Somebody touched me,' he whispered.

'Jesus,' one of his friends whispered back, 'there are hundreds of people here. I'm sure lots of them touched you.'

'No,' said Jesus, raising his voice now. 'Somebody here was sick. Very sick. Then they touched me and God made them well. I felt it. I felt the power rush out of me! Now, who was it?'

'It was me,' said a woman close by. 'I have been sick for so long. I've spent so much money on doctors. But when I touched your robe, I was healed!'

Jesus turned to the woman and smiled. He was so happy for her. 'You trusted me,' he said. 'That's good. So God has made you well.'

'Jesus,' said Jairus. 'Jesus, I don't mean to interrupt...'

But before Jairus could say another word, one of his servants called out across the crowd, 'Master, master, I have the most awful news...'

Jairus knew it even before the servant spoke.

'...your daughter is dead.'

Jesus turned from the happy woman to the sad father.

'It will be all right,' he said. 'Trust me.' Then they hurried off to Jairus' house.

When they arrived, there was another crowd—wailing and weeping in front of the house. The sad news had spread fast.

'Listen, everybody,' said Jesus. 'There's no need to cry. The girl is not dead. She's only sleeping.'

Sad tears gave way to angry laughter. 'Don't be ridiculous!' someone shouted. 'We've seen her. She's dead!'

Jesus ignored them all. He asked the girl's mother and father, and three of his friends, Peter, James and John, to come with him. Together they walked straight to where the girl was lying.

She certainly looked dead. Her eyes were closed. Her face was pale. Her skin was cold. But that didn't stop Jesus. He took her cold hand in his and called, 'Little girl, little girl, it's time to get up.'

Her skin grew warm. Her face flushed pink. And her eyelids flickered and flew open. She was alive!

And the first thing she said was, 'I'm hungry!'

'Then we'd better get you something to eat,' said Jesus.

And it was the best meal that family ever had.

The Marvellous Picnic

It wasn't long before lots of people wanted to hear Jesus talk about God. And many more wanted him to make them well. So they followed him everywhere. From town to town. From city to country. And all the way back again.

'We need a rest,' Jesus said to his friends, one day. So they took a little boat trip across Lake Galilee, hoping to camp for a while in the hills beyond. But the people were so eager to see Jesus that they raced around the shoreline to meet him on the other side!

Jesus was tired. But when he turned and saw the people following him up the hill, he stopped. 'They're like sheep without a shepherd,' he said to his friends. 'They need someone to show them the way.'

So he sat himself down—right then and there. And he started to teach.

'God loves you,' Jesus said. 'He knows what's best for you. The most amazing things can happen when you trust him.'

Jesus said a lot more than that. He taught all day, in fact. And, by then, the people were hungry.

'Philip!' Jesus called to one of his friends. 'Can you go out and buy some food for these people?'

Philip just laughed. 'There are more than five thousand of them! It would take six months' pay to feed them all.'

Then Andrew, Peter's brother, spoke up. 'There's a boy here, Jesus, who has a little food. Five loaves of bread and a couple of fish. It's not much, but it's a start.'

'So it is,' grinned Jesus, and he rubbed his hands together, as if he were about to go to work. 'Make the people sit down in little groups. Tell them we're going to have a picnic!'

Jesus' friends looked at Jesus. They looked at the boy's little lunch. They looked at the enormous crowd. Then they looked at each other and shrugged.

'All right,' they agreed. 'Whatever you say.'

Jesus smiled as he watched them go. Then he bowed his head, thanked God for the food, and started breaking it into pieces. The friends returned and began to pass out the pieces. And, to their amazement, there was plenty for the first group, and the second group, and the third group, and then every group! Plenty for everyone. More than enough to go around. So much, in fact, that there were twelve baskets full of leftovers to take home!

The people patted their tummies. They struggled to their feet. They wiped the crumbs from their mouths. And some even burped!

But all Jesus' friends could do was stare.

'It's just as I told you,' said Jesus. 'God can do the most amazing things. All we have to do is trust him.'

Then he smiled at his helpers, popped a chunk of bread into his mouth, and started off for home.

The Kind Stranger

Jesus was teaching one day when a man in the crowd asked him a question.

'Can you tell me, Jesus, what I have to do to live for ever?'

Jesus smiled. 'Love God,' he answered, 'and love your neighbour as much as you love yourself.'

'But who is my neighbour?' asked the man, hoping to trick Jesus. 'Is he just the fellow who lives next door?'

'Let me tell you a story,' Jesus said, 'and I think you will understand.'

'Once upon a time, there was a man—a man like any one of us—who was travelling from Jerusalem to Jericho. Now as you all know, that is a very dangerous road. It's twisty and it's steep, and there's no end of places for robbers and thieves to hide.

'Well, the robbers were waiting that day. And they grabbed the man. And they beat him. And they took his money and left him to die.'

'Oh dear,' sighed the crowd. They felt sorry for the man.

Jesus went on with his story.

'In a little while, another man came walking down that road—a priest, on his way home from worshipping God at the temple. He saw the dying man, and what do you think he did?'

'He helped him!' shouted someone in the crowd.

'He saved him!' shouted another.

'No!' said Jesus, firmly. 'He did not. He took one look at that poor, beaten man, crossed to the other side of the road, and walked away.'

'Oh my,' the crowd murmured.

'Wait,' Jesus continued. 'Soon another man passed by. He served God at the temple, too. So what do you think this man did when he saw the wounded traveller?'

'He ran for help!' shouted someone.

'He raised the alarm!' shouted another.

'No!' said Jesus, again. 'He did not. Just like the priest, he crossed to the other side of the road and left that poor man to die.'

'Oh no,' the crowd sighed.

'Don't worry,' said Jesus. 'For there was one more man who passed by that day. And he was a Samaritan.'

'A Samaritan?' shouted someone. 'They're different from us!'

'We hate Samaritans!' shouted another.

'And they hate us!' added a third.

'So I've heard,' nodded Jesus. 'But when

this Samaritan saw the man, he did not walk away. No. He bandaged his wounds. He loaded him on his donkey. He took him to a nearby inn. And he paid for that man to stay there until he was well.'

Jesus looked at the man who had asked him the question. 'So tell me,' he said, 'which of these men was a neighbour to the man who had been robbed?'

'The third one. The Samaritan,' the man answered.

'That's right,' Jesus smiled. 'Because my neighbour is anyone who needs my help. Now you go and help your neighbour, too.'

The Two Sisters

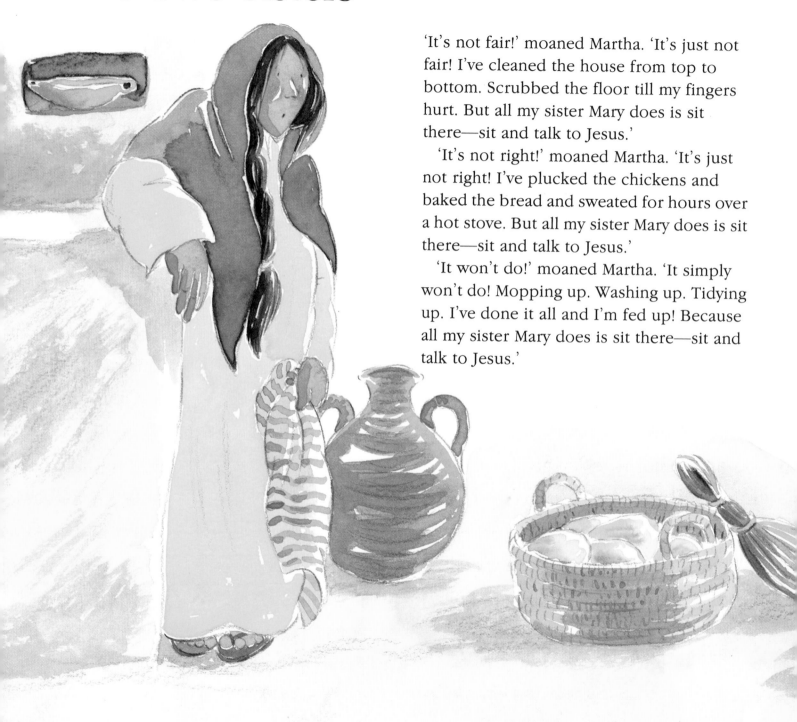

'It's not fair!' moaned Martha. 'It's just not fair! I've cleaned the house from top to bottom. Scrubbed the floor till my fingers hurt. But all my sister Mary does is sit there—sit and talk to Jesus.'

'It's not right!' moaned Martha. 'It's just not right! I've plucked the chickens and baked the bread and sweated for hours over a hot stove. But all my sister Mary does is sit there—sit and talk to Jesus.'

'It won't do!' moaned Martha. 'It simply won't do! Mopping up. Washing up. Tidying up. I've done it all and I'm fed up! Because all my sister Mary does is sit there—sit and talk to Jesus.'

'Martha,' sighed Jesus. 'Martha, my friend. I'm so glad you invited me to your house. The place is spotless. The food was delicious. But you mustn't be angry with Mary your sister. For she has made the right choice.

'Cooking and cleaning and washing up are important. But sometimes it's better to put away your brushes and cloths. To rest. And to sit and talk with me.'

'I Can See!'

'I have a question,' said one of Jesus' friends. 'There's a man here who's been blind since he was born. Did that happen because his parents did something bad?'

'No,' said Jesus. 'God doesn't punish people by making their children blind. But I'll tell you what—God can use this man's blindness to show us how powerful he is.'

And with that, Jesus walked over to the man. He knelt down. He spat on the ground. He made a little mud out of the dirt and spit. And he rubbed it on the blind man's eyes. It was very messy!

'Now go and wash your face,' Jesus said to the man. 'And you will be blind no more.'

The man washed his face, just as Jesus said. And when he shook the water from his hair and opened his eyes—he could see!

'We have a question,' said the people who gathered around him. 'Aren't you the blind man who usually goes begging for food?'

'I am,' said the man-who-used-to-be-blind.

'Then how can you see?'

'I met a man named Jesus, who rubbed mud in my eyes!'

The crowd was amazed. They were ready to cheer.

'Because a bad man made you well!' accused the teacher.

'Wait,' asked someone else. 'How could a bad man do a good thing like that?'

'That's what I want to know,' said another.

And they asked the man-who-used-to-be-blind all kinds of questions.

'Were you really blind?'

'Were you pretending?'

'Who is this Jesus, anyway?'

It was too much for the man-who-used-to-be-blind. 'Listen,' he shouted, 'I don't know the answers to all your questions, but I do know this. Once I was blind, and now I can see. Who but someone sent by God, could do a thing like that?'

A little later, as the man was sitting by himself, Jesus came to see him.

'I know it's been a hard day,' said Jesus, 'but I have a question, too. Do you believe that God sent me?'

'I do,' said the man. 'I really do!'

Jesus smiled. 'Then no more questions.'

And then someone else spoke up, 'Excuse me. I have a question, too.'

This someone was a religious teacher who didn't much like Jesus. Why? Because Jesus was too popular and didn't always agree with what the other teachers said.

'Jesus healed you? And he did it today?' the teacher asked.

'That's right,' said the man.

'Well, today is the day of rest—the special day God himself set aside. The day on which no one is allowed to work. But healing is work, surely! So how can this Jesus be on God's side if he breaks God's law?'

'I don't know,' said the man. 'But I can see!'

The Two Houses

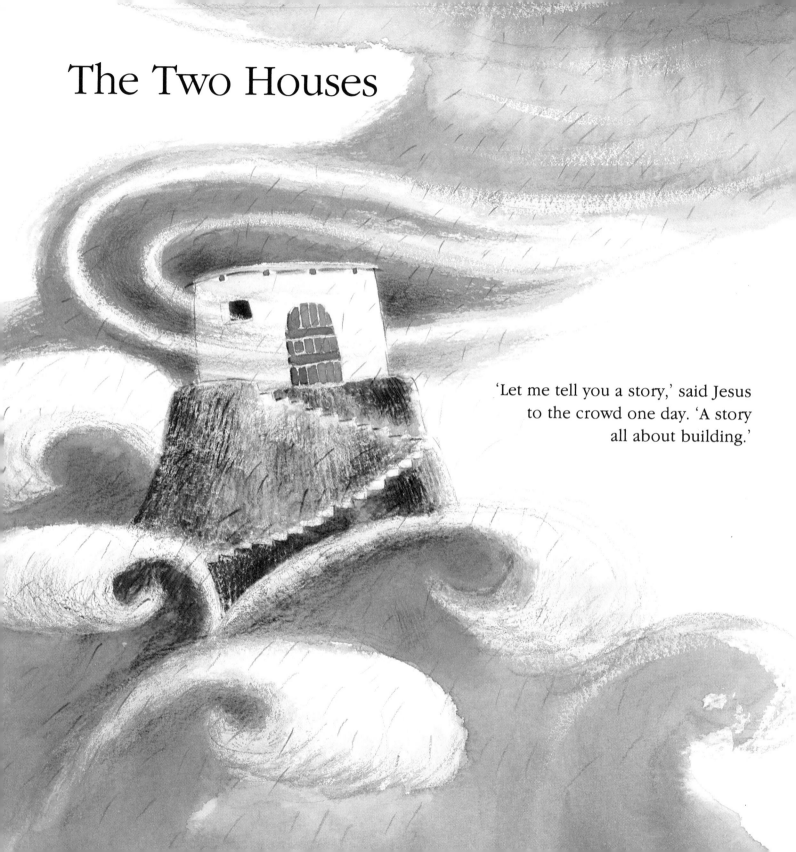

'Let me tell you a story,' said Jesus
to the crowd one day. 'A story
all about building.'

'There once was a man. A wise man, who wanted to build a house. So he found a big rock. A really big rock. And he said, "This is where I'll start."

And he dug a big hole in that really big rock, and that's where he built his house.

Then the rain came.

And the sea rose.

And the wind huffed and puffed enough to blow that house down.

But that house did not move. No, not one inch!

There was another man. A foolish man, who wanted to build a house, too.

So he found a nice beach. A soft, sandy beach.

And he said, "This is where I'll start."

And he smoothed out the sand and tossed out the shells. And that's where he built his house.

Then the rain came.

And the sea rose.

And the wind huffed and puffed enough to blow that house down.

And down it fell—with a shiver and a rumble and a crash!'

'Listen to my words,' said Jesus. 'Do what I tell you. And you will be like that first man. For the things I say are true—solid as any rock. And you can build your life upon them.'

87

The Big Party

'Come to my party!' a man said to Jesus. So Jesus went along.

But in the middle of the party, he turned to the man and said, 'You have invited all the wrong people.'

The man was surprised. 'What do you mean?' he said.

Jesus looked around the room. 'When you throw a party, you invite your important friends, your favourite relatives, and your rich neighbours, don't you?'

'Of course,' the man nodded.

'And when they throw a party, you hope they invite you, too.'

'That's right,' said the man.

'Well, I have a better idea,' said Jesus. 'The next time you throw a party, send your invitations to the poor, the crippled, the sick, and the blind.'

'But why?' asked the man, more confused than ever.

'Because none of those people could ever pay you back. They are not rich enough or well enough to throw parties of their own. But I tell you, God will be so happy with your kindness, that he will save a special seat for you at the party he plans to throw in heaven.'

One of the other guests heard this and shouted, 'Hooray for God and for everybody who gets to go to his party in heaven!'

'That reminds me of a story,' said Jesus.

'Once upon a time, there was a man—a rich man—who threw a big party for his friends. When everything was ready—the drinks and the cakes and the decorations—he told his servant to go and fetch the guests.

When the servant knocked at the first guest's house, the man met him at the door with a worried face.

"I cannot come," he said, "for I have just bought a piece of land and must go and see that it is all right."

It was just the same with the third guest.

"Can't come tonight," he explained. "Haven't you heard? I've just got married!"

When the servant reported all this to his master, the rich man was very angry.

"So they can't be bothered to come? Well, I know plenty of people who will. Go out into the streets," he ordered his servant. "And invite the poor, the crippled, the sick and the blind."

And so they came—the people no one else would invite. And it was the best party that rich man ever threw!'

Jesus looked round the room, again. 'Hooray for God!' he said. 'Rich and poor. Sick and well. He loves us all. And he wants us all to come to his party.'

When the servant knocked at the second guest's door, the man's face was much the same.

"Cows," said the man. "I've just bought some cows. One can't be too careful with cows. I must make sure they are well."

The Lost Sheep

When Jesus talked, everybody came to listen.

People who thought they were good.

And people who weren't so good, too— cheats and liars; robbers and thieves.

The people who thought they were good didn't like this one bit.

'Hey, Jesus!' they shouted.

'You say you come from God. You call him your Father. So why are you spending your time with these bad people?'

Jesus thought for a minute. 'Let me tell you a story,' he said.

'Once upon a time, there was a shepherd. A shepherd who had a hundred sheep.

He knew each of them by sight.

The white ones and the black ones.

The spotted ones and the striped ones.

The thin ones and the fat ones.

The sleek ones and the woolly ones.

And every night, after he had called them from the fields and gathered them in their pen, he would count them.

One, two, three. Four, five, six. Seven, eight, nine. And all the way to a hundred. One night, he found himself a sheep short. Ninety-seven, ninety-eight, ninety-nine, he counted.

But he never got to a hundred, because the last sheep was missing!

The shepherd looked round the pen. "It's Bramble!" he said. "It's Bramble that's gone." And what do you think he did?

Did he say to himself, "I have ninety-nine

sheep left, who cares if one is lost?'' Of course not. He cared for the missing sheep as much as for the rest. So he picked up his walking stick and off he went, across the hills and fields, looking for that lost sheep.

He looked under bushes.

He looked behind rocks.

He looked down in deep ravines.

And finally, when he had almost given up hope, he found the lost sheep, trapped in a tangle of thorns.

The shepherd shouted, "Hooray!"

Then he slung the sheep round his shoulders, and carried it safely home.

"Come to my house!" he called to his neighbours.

"Come to my house!" he called to his friends.

"My sheep was lost, and now it's found. We're going to have a party!"

'Why do I talk to people who have done bad things?' said Jesus to the crowd. 'Because God is like that shepherd. And we are all his sheep. Some stay in the pen. But some, like these robbers and thieves, wander away and get lost. So someone has to look for them and talk to them. And when they come back to him, God throws a party, too!'

The Lost Coin

'Let me tell you another story,' said Jesus to the crowd.

'Once upon a time, there was a woman. A woman who worked very hard. She worked so hard, in fact, that she managed to save ten days' pay! And she tucked it away in the safest place in her house.

One, two, three...

Four, five, six...

Seven, eight, nine...

Ten coins in all!

She knew them all by sight.

The shiny ones and the dull ones.

The thick ones and the thin ones.

The smooth ones and the dented ones.

One day, she took them out to count them.

One, two, three...

Four, five, six...

Seven, eight, nine.

But she never got to ten, because the last coin was missing!

The woman looked again inside her little box. "It's the tiny silver one," she said. "It's gone!" And what do you think she did?

Did she say to herself, "I have nine coins left, who cares if one is lost?" Of course not.

She wanted that last coin as much as the rest. So she lit a lamp and started to look.

She looked under tables and beds and chairs.

She looked under pots and pans.

She reached into crevices, cracks and nooks.

And finally she found it! Nestling in a dark corner.

The woman shouted, "Hooray!"

Then she picked up the coin and danced around the room.

92

"Come to my house!" she called to her neighbours.

"Come to my house!" she called to her friends.

"My coin was lost and now it's found. We're going to have a party!"

'And that's just what the angels do,' said Jesus, 'when someone who is far away from God turns around and does what is right.'

The Big Spender

The people who thought they were good were still not happy with Jesus. They moaned. They grumbled. They frowned.

'It's not fair,' they complained. 'Jesus spends all his time with the bad people.'

Jesus heard this and told them one more story:

'Once upon a time there was a man who had two sons. He loved them both, very much. But one day, the younger son came to him with a sad request.

"Father," the younger son said, "when you die, I will get part of your money and part of your land. The problem is, I don't want to wait. I want my money now!"

It was all the father could do to hold back his tears. But because he loved his son, he agreed, and gave him his share of the money.

That very day the son left home, money in his pocket and a big smile on his face. He didn't even say goodbye. The father just watched, wiped away a tear, and hoped that one day he would see his son again.

The son travelled to a country far, far away and spent his money just as fast as he could. He drank. He gambled. He used his money

to do many bad things—until finally the money was gone.

The son looked for a job, but the only work he could find was taking care of pigs! It was hard, dirty work, and he was so hungry sometimes that he thought about taking the pigs' food for himself. He was miserable, lonely, and sad. And then one day, he had an idea.

"The servants who take care of my father's animals are much happier than me. I'll go home, that's what I'll do. I'll tell my father how sorry I am for wasting his money. And maybe, just maybe, he'll let me become a servant and work for him."

Now what do you think the father had been doing all this time? Did he say to himself, "I have my eldest son at home with me. Who cares if my younger son is gone?" Of course not! He loved his son, even though he had gone far away. And every day, he would go out to the roadside and watch, hoping his son would return.

That's exactly where he was when the younger son hobbled home, poor and hungry. The father ran to his son and hugged him tight. And the son dropped right to his knees.

"Oh, Father," he cried. "I'm so sorry. I have wasted all your money and am no longer good enough to be your son."

"Don't be silly," said the father. "You are my son. You will always be my son. And I am so glad to have you back!" Then the father lifted his son to his feet and walked him home. He dressed him in beautiful clothes. He put gold rings on his fingers. And he threw him a big welcome home party.

When the elder son came home from work that night, he heard the party noise.

"What's happening?" he asked. And when a servant told him, he was filled with anger and ran to his father.

"It's not fair!" he shouted. "I've been a good son. I've worked hard for you all these years. But he was bad. He wasted your money. And now you're throwing him a party."

"I love you, my son," the father said. "And you have enjoyed all the good things I have. But your brother was gone, and now he's back. He was lost, and now he's found. That's why I'm having this party, because we're all back together again.' '

The Man Who Came Back

One, two, three,
  Four, five, six,
  Seven, eight, nine,
  And ten.
  There were ten lepers on the road, one day. And no one would go near them. Their fingers were numb. Their faces were scarred. They were terribly, terribly ill.
  One, two, three,
  Four, five, six,
  Seven, eight, nine,
  And ten.
  There were ten lepers on the road, one day. And Jesus came walking by. 'Jesus!' they cried. 'Oh, Jesus!' they begged. 'Save us. Please make us well!'

One, two, three,
  Four, five, six,
  Seven, eight, nine,
  And ten.
  There were ten lepers on the road, one day. And Jesus prayed for them. 'Now go!' he said. 'Go. Find a priest, and he'll tell you if you are well.'
  One, two, three,
  Four, five, six,
  Seven, eight, nine,
  And ten.
  There were ten lepers on the road, that day. And then suddenly there weren't! Their fingers were fine. Their faces like new! They were happy and healed and whole!

One, two, three,
Four, five, six,
Seven, eight,
And nine.
 Nine lepers (who weren't lepers any more!) rushed off to share their good news. But leper number ten went straight back to Jesus, to thank him for what he had done.

One, two, three,
Four, five, six,
Seven, eight, nine,
And ten.
 'I healed ten lepers on the road today,' said Jesus to the man. 'But where are the rest? Never mind, I'm just pleased that you came back to thank me!'

Jesus and the Children

'I can't see!' called a blind woman. 'Can you help me, Jesus?'

'I can't walk!' called a lame man. 'Heal me, Jesus, please!'

'He can't hear!' called a deaf man's friend. 'Touch him, Jesus, and make him well.'

They were everywhere—people with every kind of sickness. And Jesus felt sorry for them all. So he did what he could to help the crowd that day.

'I can't see,' said a little girl to her mother. 'There are too many people in the way.'

'I can't move,' said her little brother. 'We're all squashed in here.'

'What did you say?' asked their father. 'I can't hear. This crowd is so noisy!'

'Excuse me,' said their mother to one of Jesus' friends. 'We were wondering if Jesus could pray for our children.'

'Are they sick?' asked the friend.

'No,' the mother answered. 'We just wanted Jesus to ask God to watch over them and protect them.'

'I see,' said the friend impatiently. 'Well, as you have noticed, Jesus is a very busy man. He has important things to do. Lots of sick people to make well.'

'That's right!' added another of Jesus' friends. 'There are grown-ups here who need his help. He can't be bothered with children.'

'Particularly children who aren't even sick!' chimed in a third friend. 'It's just a waste of his time.'

The mother and the father and the children looked at each other. Then they looked at the ground and turned to leave. They were sad and embarrassed.

'Does this mean we won't see Jesus?' asked the little girl, rubbing the tears from her eyes.

But before her mother could answer, another voice called out across the crowd. 'Wait!' It was the voice of Jesus!

'Bring your children here,' Jesus called. 'There's nothing to be ashamed of.' And he gave his friends an unhappy look.

Jesus picked up the little boy and the little girl and set them on his lap. He gave them each a hug, and then he said, 'Listen. I want everybody to listen. Particularly my friends. You must never keep the children away from me. They are as important to me as anyone else. And I want to be their friend, too.

'Don't you see? God wants us all to be like these children. To love him like a father. To trust him completely. And to long to be with him.'

Then Jesus prayed for the children, hugged them one more time, and sent them beaming back to their parents.

Jesus and the Taxman

'Jesus is coming!' somebody shouted. 'Jesus is coming to Jericho!' And everybody ran to meet him.

Well, almost everybody. For there was one man—one wee little man—who did not run to meet Jesus. And his name was Zacchaeus.

It's not that Zacchaeus didn't want to see Jesus. He did. He really did. But, not only was Zacchaeus short, he was also afraid of the crowd. Not many people liked him, you see. Partly because he was a tax collector. But mostly because he collected more taxes than he was supposed to—and kept what was left for himself.

'Jesus is here!' somebody shouted. 'Jesus is here in Jericho!' And everybody cheered as he walked through the city gates.

Well, almost everybody. For Zacchaeus did not feel like cheering at all. He wanted to see Jesus. He really did. But how could he walk out there in front of all those people he'd cheated? And what would they do if they got hold of him?

Then Zacchaeus had an idea. There were trees by the city gates—tall, leafy trees. If he could sneak behind the crowd and climb one of those trees, he could see Jesus—and not be seen himself!

So off he went—out of his house and through the empty streets. And because the crowd was watching Jesus, he had no trouble at all slipping behind them and shinning up a tree.

'Come, eat at my house!' somebody shouted. 'Come, eat at my house, Jesus!' And because it was a great honour to host someone as important as Jesus, everybody shouted at once.

Well, almost everybody. For there was one man—one wee little man—who kept his mouth shut and tried hard not to rustle the branches.

'Thank you very much,' said Jesus. 'You are very kind. But I have already decided where I will eat my dinner.'

Then Jesus looked straight at the trees and called, 'Zacchaeus! Zacchaeus, come down! I'm eating at your house today.'

'Zacchaeus?' somebody shouted. 'Jesus is eating with Zacchaeus? He's the worst man in town. There must be some mistake!' And everybody moaned and groaned.

Well, almost everybody. One man—one wee little man—climbed down from the tree, as shocked as the rest. Why would someone as good as Jesus want to eat with someone bad like him? But he was happy, too. Happier than he'd been for a long, long time. And so, with a smile spreading across his face, Zacchaeus led Jesus to his house.

'What are they saying?' somebody whispered. 'What are they doing in there?' And everybody gathered around the taxman's door.

That's when Zacchaeus threw open his door with a bang!

'Greetings, everyone!' he shouted. 'I have an announcement to make. I've been talking with my new friend, Jesus, and realize that there are a few things I need to change. I've cheated some of you. I admit that. And I want you to know that I'm sorry. So sorry, in fact, that I will pay you back four times more than I stole from you! What's more, I intend to sell half of what I own and give the money to the poor!'

The crowd was shocked. Never, in their whole lives, had they seen anyone change like that! They stood there with their mouths wide open. And nobody said a thing.

Well, almost nobody.

'Don't you see?' said Jesus to the crowd. 'God has sent me to share his love with everybody—even those who have done some very bad things. That's what I have done. And now Zacchaeus loves God, too.'

That's when the crowd began to cheer. Jesus. And Zacchaeus. And the whole town of Jericho.

Everybody.

The Great Parade

'Let's go to Jerusalem!' said Jesus to his friends. 'I have something important to do there.'

So they went. And when they could just see the city from a nearby hillside, Jesus said, 'Let's have a parade!'

Jesus' friends were surprised. 'A parade?' they wondered. 'Why a parade?' But no one said anything, because Jesus was already busy giving instructions.

'I want two of you to borrow a donkey,' he said. 'Tell the owner I need it. He'll understand.'

When the two friends returned with the donkey, Jesus hopped on its back, gently nudged its sides, and started down the hill. His friends followed close behind.

'Hooray for Jesus!' they shouted. 'Jesus is King!'

Down, down, down they rode, towards the city gate. And the closer they got, the more people joined them.

'It's Jesus the Teacher!' someone called.

'It's Jesus the Healer!' called someone else.

'Three cheers for Jesus!' called one and all.

Soon there were people everywhere, marching along with the parade and shouting from the roadside.

Some took off their coats and laid them in front of the donkey. Others cut palm branches from the trees and waved them about. There were hundreds, maybe thousands, clapping and dancing and shouting their way through the city gates. Everyone was happy!

Well, almost everyone. Some of the religious leaders didn't like Jesus. They were jealous, because the ordinary people were so fond of him. And when they saw the parade, they frowned.

'Wait just a minute!' they called. 'You can't have a parade here. Tell your friends to be quiet, Jesus.'

But Jesus just laughed. 'Tell them to be quiet? Impossible!' Then he turned to look at the crowd.

'Can't you see?' he said. 'There's so much happiness here that even if I could make the people quiet, the stones in the street would jump up and shout for joy!'

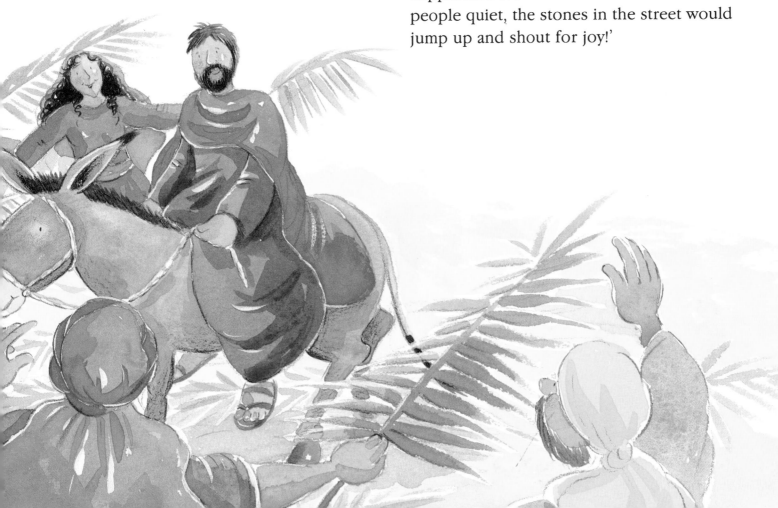

An Important Meal

Jesus and his twelve friends sat down to eat. There was lamb and bread and wine. A nice meal. But Jesus was sad.

'What's the matter, Jesus?' asked one of his friends.

'I have to go away tomorrow,' Jesus sighed. 'And I will miss you very much.'

Jesus' friends were surprised. 'Where are you going?' they asked.

'I am going to be with my Father in heaven,' he whispered. 'I am going to die.'

Now Jesus' friends were sad, too.

'There are people here in Jerusalem who do not like me,' Jesus explained. 'They do not agree with what I teach. They do not believe I come from God. And tomorrow they will arrest me and hurt me and nail me to a cross and kill me.'

'No!' said Jesus' friends. 'They will not do that. We will not let them!'

Jesus looked at them sadly. 'One of you has already taken money from them and agreed to help them catch me.'

Jesus' friends stared at each other.

'Well, it's not me!' said one.

'It's not me,' said another.

But one of them—a man named Judas— just looked at Jesus, then stood up and walked out of the room.

'Let him go,' Jesus told the others. 'We have something more important to do.'

And with that, Jesus took a chunk of bread and said a thank-you prayer.

'I will never forget you,' he said to his friends. 'And I don't want you to forget me either.' Then he broke the bread in half and passed it round. 'This is my body,' he said. 'I give it up for you. Take it and eat it and remember me.'

Then he took a cup of wine and said a thank-you prayer for that, as well.

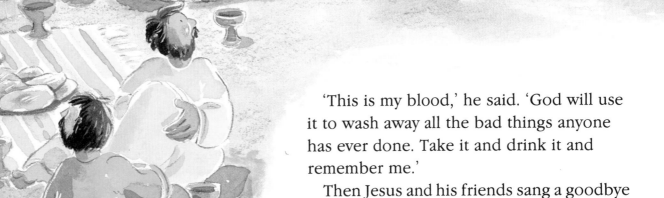

'This is my blood,' he said. 'God will use it to wash away all the bad things anyone has ever done. Take it and drink it and remember me.'

Then Jesus and his friends sang a goodbye song and walked out together into the night.

A Dreadful Day

When Jesus and his friends had finished their goodbye meal, they walked to a garden to pray. That's where Jesus' enemies found him.

The men had torches and clubs and sticks. They were very frightening. And right in front was Judas, who had been one of Jesus' friends.

Judas crept up to Jesus and kissed him on the cheek. 'This is the man you want!' said Judas. 'Arrest him!' Jesus looked very sad.

Jesus' friends were scared. Most of them ran away. But not Peter. He pulled out a sword and started swinging it about.

'Put your sword away,' said Jesus. 'This is not the time for fighting. I have to go with them. God wants me to.'

So they grabbed Jesus, and dragged him before the religious leaders—the ones who were jealous of him. His trial took all night.

'He says he will destroy our temple,' said one man.

'He says he is a king,' said another.

'He's a troublemaker!' said one and all.

None of this was true, of course. But it didn't matter, because the leaders had already made up their minds. Jesus was different from them. Jesus wouldn't do what they said. So Jesus would have to die.

They beat Jesus. They hit him hard. Then they took away his clothes, put an old robe round his shoulders, and jammed a crown made of thorns on his head. And while the blood ran down his forehead, they called him names and made fun of him. 'So you think you're a king?' they laughed. 'Well, look at you now!'

Jesus never said a word. His body hurt, his heart was breaking, but he never said a word.

They took a cross, next, made of heavy wood, and they laid it on his back. 'Move along!' they shouted, and they led him through the city. Some people cried when they saw him. Others cheered. But all of them followed, as he lugged that cross through the city gates and up a nearby hill.

When they got to the top, they laid Jesus on the cross and nailed him to it. It hurt so much. Then they raised the cross, so that everyone could see, and they left him there to die.

A thief, hanging next to him, was afraid. But Jesus talked to him and helped him feel better.

Jesus' mother was there, too, standing in

the crowd. So Jesus called to one of his friends, 'Take care of her for me, will you, John? She's your mother, now.'

But most of the faces in the crowd were not so kind. 'You saved other people,' someone laughed, 'so why can't you save yourself?'

Jesus knew why. It wasn't because his enemies had won. It was because God wanted him there—to take away all the bad things anyone had ever done.

Soon the sky grew dark and the earth shook. It was as if God's own heart was breaking. And then it happened.

'It's done,' Jesus whispered. And in the sadness and the dark, he died.

A Happy Day

It was very early. The birds were still in bed. And the sun had yet to open its bright eye on the world. The sky was grey and grainy. The air was cold. And three women walked slowly towards the graveyard.

Jesus was buried there. And the women were coming to visit his grave.

They talked in sad whispers. They cried. They held each other's hands. Jesus had been dead for three days, and they missed him very much.

Just as they reached the graveyard, however, some surprising things happened. The ground began to shake. The air began to tremble. And, quick as lightning, an angel flashed down from heaven and rolled the stone away from Jesus' tomb!

Everything went quiet. The ground stopped moving. But the women shook with fear.

'Don't be afraid,' the angel said. 'Come and see. The tomb is empty. Jesus is alive!'

Arm in arm, the women crept past the angel and into the tomb. The sheets were still there—the sheets they had wrapped round his dead body. But Jesus himself was gone!

'Where is he?' asked the women. 'What have you done with him?'

'I told you,' smiled the angel. 'He's not dead any more. He's come back to life. And he wants you to tell all his friends.'

The women looked at each other. They didn't know whether to laugh or cry. They could hardly believe it—that is until they hurried out of the tomb and ran straight into Jesus.

'Oh, Jesus!' they cried. 'It's true. You are alive!' And they fell at his feet, amazed!

'There's no need to be afraid any more,' he said. 'God has made everything all right. But I have a job for you. I want you to tell the rest of my friends that I am alive. Tell them I will meet them on the seashore, in Galilee, where all our adventures started.'

The women waved goodbye and hurried off to Jerusalem. The birds were singing now. The sun's bright eye was wide open. And they had the most amazing story to tell.

Goodbye at Last

When Jesus came back from the dead, he appeared many times and in many different places.

His friends were hiding in a locked room, so the men who killed Jesus couldn't find them. And, all of a sudden, Jesus was there in the room with them! They were frightened. They were confused. They thought he was a ghost!

But Jesus said, 'Don't be afraid. It's me. It really is. Look, here are the marks the nails made in my hands, and the cut the soldier's sword made in my side.'

Then Jesus joined them for dinner and ate a bit of food—to prove that he wasn't a ghost at all.

A few weeks later, his friends were out fishing. They couldn't catch a thing. Then, all of a sudden, they heard a voice from the shore, 'Throw your nets on the other side of the boat!' And when they did, they caught more fish than their boats could hold.

'Wait a minute,' said Peter. 'This is the same thing that happened all those years ago, when Jesus asked us to follow him. It must be him on the beach!' And, all of a sudden, Peter jumped into the sea—clothes and all—and swam back to shore.

The other friends followed as fast as they could and when they arrived, they discovered that Jesus had been doing some fishing of his own. Jesus was cooking fish over a hot fire. They smelled delicious!

'Dry yourselves off. Sit down by the fire,' Jesus said. 'Let's have a picnic right here on the beach.'

A few more weeks passed and, at last, the time came for Jesus to leave—to go to heaven and be with God his Father. So he took one last walk with his friends, up a hill near the Sea of Galilee where their adventures together had begun.

'I've got to go now,' Jesus said, 'and there is something I want you to do. Tell my story to the world. Start in Jerusalem, and don't stop until everybody has the chance to follow me.

'And, if you ever feel scared or alone, don't worry. Just talk to me, and I'll be with you. I promise.'

Then, all of a sudden, a cloud wrapped itself round Jesus and carried him into the sky. His friends stood and stared, their mouths open, their eyes filled with tears, until two angels appeared and spoke to them.

'Don't be sad,' the angels said. 'One day, Jesus will come back—in the clouds—just as you've seen him go.'

So off the friends went, down the hill—and into the whole world, to tell the story of Jesus.

Sharing stories with a crowd

Storytelling was never meant to be a one-way street. At its best, it is a kind of dialogue, something that happens between a storyteller and an audience. One way to encourage that is to give your audience specific ways to participate in the story. On the opposite page you will find a few suggestions for getting groups of children (or adults) more involved in the stories from *The Storyteller Bible*.

These suggestions might spark ideas for how you could use some other stories from *The Storyteller Bible*. Above all, have fun with the storytelling and if an idea doesn't work, try something else instead. Enjoy yourself—and those in your audience will enjoy themselves too.

In the Beginning (page 10)

This works well with a large group. Choose someone to play Adam, someone to play Eve, and three others for the sun, the moon and the stars. Adam and Eve lie down on the floor, with the sun, moon and stars around them. At the appropriate time in the story, they leap up and act out their parts—a big, bright 'Ta-da!' for the sun, perhaps, arms in the shape of a crescent for the moon and twinkling fingers for the stars.

Don't leave the others out either! Before the story begins, divide the crowd into four groups: the growing things, the flying things, the swimming things, and the crawling things. As you tell the story, let them act out their chosen plant or animal part at the right time. This can get noisy and crazy and wild—but it also can echo the joy and excitement of creation. Finally, let everyone calm down so that everything is ready—good and ready—for you to introduce them to Adam and Eve.

The Fall of Jericho (page 38)

This is another good story for a large crowd. Divide the audience into three groups: one on the left (the people of Jericho), one on the right (the Israelites), and one in the middle (the wall!), facing the Israelite group. The 'wall' should link arms or do anything to make it more wall-like! As you tell the story, encourage the groups to act out their parts as they come. (And don't give away the line about the wall being thick too soon.)

David the Giant-Killer (page 44)

Choose a small boy or girl to play David. Give them a long sock, folded in two, to swing round their head and let fly. Choose someone a little bigger for King Saul. Sit that person on a chair (throne) in front of the crowd, and drape a large coat or jumper over their shoulders (this can double as armour later and should dwarf little David).

Finally, choose someone very big for Goliath (I often go for an adult). Give that person something pointed to wave as a spear—a pencil, perhaps! As you tell the story, let the characters act out the parts, and perhaps even repeat their lines after you.

Jonah the Groaner (page 52)

This one is very simple. Ask the audience to groan, softly at first and then louder and louder, every time they hear the phrase 'Jonah groaned'. I always do a bit of editing at the end of this story and finish up with one last 'And what did Jonah do? Jonah groaned!' so the listeners can have a really good groan at the end.

The Storm on the Lake (page 74)

Ask the audience to rock gently back and forth. They are the waves on the lake, and they need to keep rocking throughout the story—gently at first and then more wildly as the storm strikes. Then calm them down, as Jesus stills the storm, and finally make them rock gently again.